# Adventurous Lady

*Margaret Brent of Maryland*

# Adventurous Lady

## MARGARET BRENT
### *of Maryland*

By
Dorothy Fremont Grant

*Illustrated by* Douglas Grant

HILLSIDE EDUCATION

Cover and interior book design by Mary Jo Loboda

ISBN: 978-0-9991706-3-2

Hillside Education
475 Bidwell Hill Road
Lake Ariel, PA 18436
www.hillsideeducation.com

# Contents

# Adventurous Lady

*Margaret Brent of Maryland*

NOTE: The historical dates in this story follow the Maryland Archives. These are according to the Old Style Calendar by which New Year's Day was March 25th, the Feast of the Annunciation

# 1.

# Just Between Ourselves

WHEN Margaret Brent arrived on this earth in the dawn of the seventeenth century—1601 to be exact—there was no reason to suppose she would be remembered after her life was over. Naturally she was very important to her parents, as all babies are, especially so because since their marriage in 1594 they had had six sons. A daughter was a welcome change.

Fulke was the eldest son, then came Richard, Giles (pronounced as though the G were a J), William, Edward, and George. Margaret began a new trend. Six sisters followed her, Mary, Catherine, Elizabeth, Eleanor, Jane, and Ann.

It was all unusually expensive because the Brents were Catholics. They lived in Gloucestershire, England, at a time when harsh laws were enforced against anyone who was not a member of the Church of England. This was the State church established by Parliament a good many years before Margaret or her brothers were born.

England had been a Catholic country for about fifteen centuries. It was called "Mary's Dowry." Even an English king, Henry VIII, had been given by the Pope the title "Defender of the Faith," but it soon turned out that the English monarch defended the faith of the Church of England which was not what the Pope had had in mind.

Elizabeth I was Queen when Margaret was born. She didn't begin to be as pretty and nice as Elizabeth II who is Queen today. And her laws against the Catholics especially were crushing and cruel. She died on the twenty-fourth of March, 1603 (which date at that time was the last day of the year as people then used the Old Style calendar), and James VI of Scotland hurried down from Edinburgh to London to be crowned James I of England. James had very little use for Elizabeth, whom many English people loved, because she had chopped off his mother's head. She was Mary Queen of Scots.

But he also had very little use for his mother's religion, Catholicism. And when he became King of England he decided that Elizabeth's laws were not strict enough. Elizabeth believed she had put teeth into the penal laws, as they were called; James decided to make the teeth bite.

Rich people had terrible fines to pay. They were much worse than our income taxes. Poor people who simply would not go to the Church Parliament had set up were put in jail or whipped in public. But with the rich people, especially people of the peerage and of what is called blue blood (which always runs red when they cut themselves), it was a different story. They paid and paid and paid. And if they didn't pay promptly, two thirds of their lands, their houses, and their valuables were confiscated by the Crown.

This is what happened to Sir Richard Brent, Lord of Stoke and Admington, when his daughter Margaret was a young woman. And it turned him into a bitter old man.

The first and foremost fine that had to be paid by every Englishman who would not attend the State church was £20 per lunar month—of which there are thirteen in a twelve-month calendar year. Sir Richard had to pay for himself, for his wife Lady Elizabeth who was a descendant of King Edward III, and for his thirteen children £300 each lunar month—about $1,500 in our present-day dollars, which amounted to $19,500 every year!

There were any number of other fines: if Catholics were not married by a minister of the Church of England, if their babies were not baptized in that church, if they sent their children to the Continent for their education in seminaries and convents, if they were not buried in Protestant cemeteries—all of these "if's" were subject to heavy fines. And Catholics especially could never be lawyers, doctors, judges, or officers in the army or navy. They had to stay within five to ten miles of their homes, too, and couldn't travel about the country freely. You can see how very expensive it was to remain a Catholic in the England of that day, and how frustrating not to be able to do what one wanted to do. Sir Richard Brent with his large family had a hard time of it.

Early one April morning in 1632, seven years after King James had died (his son Charles was now King), Sir Richard called his family together in the hall of Admington Manor. It was a rainy day and a big fire was blazing on the hearth. But when Giles went to add another log to it, just to make it give out even more heat, his father stopped him.

"We have got to economize," he said, "if we are to keep ourselves together under this ancestral roof. Better a little fire than none."

Giles dropped the log and brushed off his hands.

"This is precisely why I have called you together," his father went on, and there was a tone of grumble and irritation in his voice. "I want to keep us under this roof. And I am beside myself with worry. Now you, my daughters, will have to reconcile yourselves to making do with what gowns and cloaks you have. I know not when I shall be able to afford another stitch for any of you.

"And you, my beloved," he went on, turning to Lady

Elizabeth who sat beside him near the fire, "will have to curtail our table. No more expensive boar's head and pheasant and squab. You feed us beef and kidney pie, and," he turned again to his children, "see that we have no complaints about the reduced fare at our table. No more imported wines. And you, my sons, will have to cut back on your sports, reduce the stable and the kennel, less running to the hounds, and see to it you make your wardrobes last longer. We will also have to cut down on the servants. Our tenants can remain, our personal maids and valets will have to go, and the scullery maid, too."

Now and then Sir Richard's voice broke as he gave out this ultimatum. He found it hard to look his family squarely in the eye.

Richard and Jane were not there. They had married and had their own establishments and troubles, although Jane, living in Paris, was not hindered in matters of faith. Ann, the youngest, just past five, was upstairs with her governess whom Sir Richard said would also have to go. Catherine and Eleanor were at school with the Augustinians in Bruges, and George was at St. Omer's in France where William, now home, had also been educated.

"Are you bringing the others home from school?" Margaret asked her father.

"Not if I can possibly help it," he replied quickly and a bit crossly. He had made many sacrifices to educate his children, praying in his heart that at least one son would become a priest and one daughter a nun. There was no evidence of either vocation, which was a great disappointment to Sir Richard.

William had done his best. Though he had no vocation for the priesthood, he had written some scholarly pamphlets about the Catholic faith. Sir Richard had been pleased and proud. But every time William boldly published and circulated one of his pamphlets he was put into prison. And there he had so much idle time on his hands that he wrote more pamphlets. He had his own personal disappointment, too: he had wanted to be a lawyer but he couldn't because he would not give up his religion.

After Sir Richard's little talk, which was not easy for him or Lady Elizabeth, or any of the family, everyone felt very depressed and downcast. Lady Elizabeth, who had been in frail health ever since Ann was born, was about to excuse herself and take to her bed for the rest of the day when the houseman announced a caller.

He was the Earl of Warwick.

All the blood left Sir Richard's face when he heard that name. His eyes silently spoke the fear in his heart.

"One thing I omitted to tell you all," he said, the words coming out between his teeth as though spoken with his last breath, "I am now six months behind in my fines."

Lady Elizabeth sank back in her chair, weak with foreboding. "So it has come even to us—our evil day," she said faintly.

As long as Margaret lived she never forgot the humiliating scene that followed.

The Earl of Warwick, Lord Robert Rich, entered the hall as though making an important entrance in a stage play. He bowed low to Lady Elizabeth, then to Sir Richard, and only slightly to Fulke, Giles, William, Margaret, Mary, and Elizabeth.

It turned out that he came at the special command of the King. This was intended as a compliment to Sir Richard since

*Lord Robert Rich, the King's messenger, demands more payments from Margaret's father*

he was a member of the peerage. But, actually, he came to collect the fines. And if Sir Richard would not pay at once . . .

"I've simply not got the wherewithal at present," Sir Richard told him bluntly when he had stated his business. "Tell His Majesty—"

"His Majesty," interrupted the Earl rudely, "commanded me to bring no messages or excuses, only—"

He stopped suddenly because he was so embarrassed. He had a great respect for Sir Richard and regretted very much the errand that brought him to Admington Manor. The King had told him if the Manor had to be sacrificed, he, Lord Robert Rich, could have it for himself. Although he thought it much more cheerful and homey than his gloomy old Warwick Castle, he truly did not want to take it away from Sir Richard. As he stood before the master of the Manor, who was seated in his old Venetian chair, his painful gouty foot up on a stool, he wished sincerely that the King had sent someone else on this unpleasant business.

He fiddled nervously with his huge gauntlet gloves, and almost dropped them when Sir Richard broke the silence with a booming voice.

"Only what!" he demanded harshly. He was proud and belligerent.

Margaret had been watching her father closely. His brave defiance thrilled her, but she felt a terrific lump in her heart, for she knew it would be useless.

"The fact of the matter is," resumed the Earl of Warwick, looking intently at the toe of his shoe, "His Majesty requires payment within the month, or his searchers will confiscate your valuables, two thirds of your land,s and this manor house as well. Meanwhile . . .

He stopped suddenly to give Lady Elizabeth time to recover her composure. She had nearly fainted away (though in the seventeenth century ladies swooned) and Sir Richard's face had turned an alarming shade of purple.

The very injustice of the command infuriated him. His family had held his land originally under the abbots of Glastonbury whose abbey was founded in 708. William the Conqueror (1066, remember?) had listed his ancestor Odo de Brent, Lord of Cassington, in the Domesday Book. It seemed utterly incredible that under the English bill of rights, the Magna Carta, the Crown could step in and do this to him only because he was being loyal to the religion of his ancestors.

Fulke and Giles and William turned their backs upon the Earl of Warwick and looked out the long windows of Admington Manor toward the Forest of Dean and the meadows close by. Here their father's herd of Cotswold sheep were contentedly grazing, unaware they would soon belong to the Earl instead of to Sir Richard Brent. Margaret and Mary and Elizabeth hovered about their mother who was making a heroic effort to show no further emotion.

Sir Richard's gout gave him a nasty twinge as in a voice of hot temper he broke the heavy silence.

"Meanwhile!" he prompted the Earl.

"Meanwhile," the unhappy visitor resumed as he stood very stiff and straight with his left hand on the hilt of his sword, "His Majesty instructs me to conduct your son William to the Gatehouse at Westminster as a hostage for your payment of your fines."

"William, eh? Ah, yes, William. He will be no stranger to His Majesty's hospitality."

"He will be kept under heavy guard," continued the Earl,

"until your arrears have been paid or until you have turned over Admington Manor to me."

"To you! So that's it! Zounds!"

William turned quickly from the window. "Permit me," he told the Earl, "to gather my writing equipment, my quills and ink and paper, also a change of linen, my nightshirt and another suit of clothes, my long cloak and a few bottles of wine, and I will go with you at once."

He tried to make it sound as though he were off for a jolly weekend with the Earl at Warwick Castle instead of going to prison. He did not want his father to think he minded.

As William spoke, Margaret stood biting her tongue. Her good sense told her to keep her lips closed, to say not one word, but her fastbeating heart gave her tongue many sharp words to say which she would dearly have enjoyed hurling at the Earl. But then she, too, might be carried off to prison.

She felt the Earl's eyes on her; sensed that he knew just about what she would like to say and that he hoped she wouldn't say it. She had little sympathy for him: she could not forget his grandfather's false testimony at a trial long ago that had cost the Bishop of Rochester, John Fisher, his head.

Turning sharply to the Earl, she said, "You will excuse my mother, my sisters, and myself. Your errand seems completed and my mother is not well."

With that she put her hand under her mother's elbow, nodded to Mary to take the other one and followed by Elizabeth carrying her mother's shawl, the ladies of Admington Manor left the hall in silent dignity.

# 2.

# Another Home, Another Visitor

THE Brents were living in Larke Stoke now. It was a much smaller house than Admington Manor from which they had moved a year ago, and about five miles from it, on the edge of what formerly had been Sir Richard's large tract of land. In generations gone by Larke Stoke was the home of the superintendent of the estate, now it was the residence of Sir Richard, himself, and of his family. Margaret and Mary had taken the upstairs sitting room on the front of the house for their own apartment, using it at night for their bedroom and by day for their indoor activities. Today they were sewing busily, once again remodeling and making over their summer wardrobes for the second time.

Margaret put aside her sewing.

"My fingers are so cold I cannot hold my needle," she told Mary as she left her low stool by the window, where she had excellent light for her work, and crossed to the fireplace.

On top of the brass coal scuttle lay a pair of soiled loose gloves. Margaret put them on, then lifted a big chunk of cannel coal and dropped it into the grate on the pink ashes which were giving out no heat whatever. In no time the oils in the coal caught fire. Sparks began to fly up the chimney; the flames grew higher and higher.

Margaret turned her back to the blaze, smiled appreciatively and said, "Come, Mary, come toast yourself. You look blue with cold."

"I feel like an iceberg," said Mary as she clutched her shawl tightly around her shoulders and stood beside her sister. "But you know we can't afford to be warm as this," she mildly scolded.

"Bother the expense!" said Margaret. "If we got the vapors it would cost Papa dearly for the doctor and his prescriptions, or dearer yet should we die."

"I doubt we should," Mary replied. "We're a hardy family except for poor dear Mama. I worry so about her. Will she ever be better? "

"Just as soon as these damp spring days are over," Margaret said cheerfully, "and we can get Mama out into the warm sunshine she will pick up, you will see."

"You said the same thing last spring."

"But last spring was another story—we were moving, and that nearly broke her heart."

"And Papa's, too. Everything about Papa has worsened so—his gout, his temper—he has aged."

"Yes, I know. He just cannot reconcile himself to living in a house he once provided for his servant. If he would forget to call this really comfortable home his 'miserable little hut' he would begin to feel better."

"It hurts me clear through," Mary said, "to see Papa so crushed. All for lack of money, really. Oh, if only when Giles went out to Virginia back in '25, he could have laid out the tobacco plantations! By now they would have yielded so much they could have relieved the burden Papa carries."

"But the failure was not of his doing, remember," Margaret said, turning around to face the fire and warm her other side.

Both sisters were silent as they remembered with what high hopes Giles had gone to Virginia the very year King James had died. But it did not work out.

Perhaps the Virginians thought that Giles wanted to repeat the attempt of Sir George Calvert to plant a colony as a refuge for his persecuted fellow Catholics. Sir George did start a colony in Nova Scotia, but the winters were so long and cold, so many got sick and died, that he took all the survivors to Virginia, never thinking they would be unwelcome because of their faith. But he was quickly disillusioned.

Sir George Calvert was distantly related to the Brents. He had become a Catholic while serving King James as Secretary of State. The King had liked him so much that although he accepted his resignation he gave him the title Baron of Baltimore and a large estate in Ireland as well as a charter for a colony in the New World. Sir George died at the early age of fifty-three, just as he was about to have a new charter—this time for Maryland—from King James's son, King Charles, then reigning in England. And yet it was this same King Charles who had taken from the Brents their land and home.

As if speaking her thoughts aloud, Mary said, "Isn't it strange, Margaret, how His Majesty favors some of our faith and not others?"

"We mustn't sicken ourselves with these thoughts," Margaret told her sister, putting her arm around Mary's shoulders. "If we let our resentment live over this royal contradiction we will have a festering within ourselves worse than any chill for lack of warmth. It is this which is truly killing our dear Papa . . . and yet . ."

Mary drew away from her sister a little to look at her curiously.

"I know when you speak in that tone you have a tremendous idea in mind," she said quietly. "What is it this time, Margaret? Out with it."

"I have been talking with Giles and Fulke. They want to go out to Maryland this year when our new Lord Baltimore, Cecilius, sends his brother Leonard with a group of settlers.

And—and—this I did not tell you, Mary, but a week ago I had a letter from Leonard."

"Why should you have told me?" Mary asked her. "Leonard has been writing you on and off since he was a moon-eyed little boy in his first knee breeches. Someday, when Mama is feeling better, I am going to ask her to put on paper just how it is that we are related to the Calverts . . . I have always wondered. The kinship is distant, I know well. Does it come through Mama's people the Reeds, or from Papa's side? In any event, what makes you feel you should have told me of a letter from young Leonard? "

Margaret flushed a little and her eyes smiled.

"I guess we'd better stop calling him 'young Leonard' from now on because he will be Governor General of Maryland. I didn't tell you because—well—now Mary don't dare laugh . . . in his last letter Leonard asked me to marry him, and he will be here any day for my answer."

"Well, mercy on us! You've given him that answer over and over since he first came here as a lad with his parents." Once more she looked at her sister, puzzled. "You're not taking him seriously this time, are you?"

Margaret turned her back to the fire and gazed across the room, out the windows.

"This time," she said slowly, "Leonard is taking it seriously. He wants me to marry him and go out to Maryland with him—Lady Calvert, no less. He says"—she paused, bit her lip, turned to Mary and looked right into her dark eyes—"he says he loves me, Mary. That he will never love anyone else. That . . ."

Mary went back to their sewing at the window. Slowly she sat down on the cushioned stool and picked up the dress she had been working on. She held her needle up to the light, squinted as she guided a strand of thread through the tiny eye. Then, knotting the other end of the thread, she began again her fine stitches in the newly turned hem of the old dress.

"I have not the right to ask . . . but if you would . . . What are you going to tell him? "

"You shouldn't ask," Margaret agreed. "I shouldn't have tempted you."

"Well, if you've been talking it over with Fulke and Giles . . ."

"I haven't been talking of this with them. Leonard wants them to send indentured servants with him if they cannot go themselves. Cecilius will give two hundred acres for every indenture. Tobacco plantations. You follow me?"

Mary dropped her sewing in her lap and looked up quickly. "Why has all this been kept from me? " she asked.

"Because you are afraid of the ocean and the Indians."

"You speak in riddles! We are safe from both here. What has that to do with it? "

"I, too, would like us, you and me, to send servants to Maryland, and I have feared to ask you until now."

"You and I? Margaret! You can't mean . . . You mean . . ."

"Yes. I mean in time to come perhaps we, too, will go out there to make a new life. Will you think of it, Mary? Giles is definitely planning on it."

"And Fulke?" cut in Mary. "How can Fulke think of such a thing? He is Papa's oldest son, his heir."

"Which would not prevent him from owning plantations in Maryland which Giles can manage."

"True. It's all well and good for our brothers to join this venture if they wish, and it would be a wonderful help for Papa. But my goodness me, Margaret, you can't be serious about going to Maryland yourself? And I with you? Or—I was forgetting—are you going to tell Leonard?"

Just here, before Mary could finish her question, Tidd, who had been born at Admington Manor and retained in service to the Brents over all other servants, knocked on the door. He announced the arrival of Leonard Calvert, who was waiting in the drawing room. "He has asked especially to see you, ma'am," Tidd concluded, speaking directly to Margaret.

"Both of us will be down presently," Margaret replied. After Tidd had closed the door, she added to Mary, "Come, tidy yourself as I shall do and face Leonard with me. I do not wish to be left alone with him." She smiled wryly as she took her magenta red velvet gown from the wardrobe. "Does that answer your question? "

"The answer would be more convincing," said Mary with her tongue in her cheek, "if you were not planning to put on your very best gown to meet him!"

"It may be my best now," Margaret replied, her voice muffled as she pulled two full petticoats over her head, "but you know last year I was on the verge of giving it away because it does nothing at all for my hair. That's the trouble with having red hair."

"I've told you a dozen times it is not red but titian," said Mary with slight irritation. "Our late Queen had red hair, fire red."

"And black teeth," put in Margaret.

"The color of your hair is truly beautiful. Ladies by the score would give their eyeteeth to have it. Now hush up and hurry."

When they reached the drawing room, Leonard was in earnest conversation with Fulke and Giles. He broke from them abruptly and came toward the two sisters with a cordial greeting to both, but with eyes only for Margaret.

"I say, girls," remarked Giles, "Leonard is about ready to sail. Says his vessel, the *Ark* has been completely overhauled, and the venture thus far so popular Cecilius is put to it to provide another ship."

"Much smaller than the *Ark*," added Leonard. "The little *Dove* is less than half her size."

"What matter that?" asked Mary. "Is not the *Ark* twice the size of the *Mayflower* which landed the pilgrim Puritans in New England? "

At this mention of the new England pilgrims Leonard told them of the provision for religious freedom contained in Cecilius' instructions to the Maryland colonists. Like the Puritan leaders, Lord Baltimore wanted his settlers to be free from religious persecution, but this freedom was not only for his fellow Catholics. Everyone would be at liberty to worship according to his conscience. The Catholics would be able to have Mass and to practice their faith. The Church of England people—actually of those who had signed for the voyage they were in the majority—could have their ministers and services too. And any other form of Christian worship would be allowed.

"Cecilius sees no reason," Leonard said proudly, "why men of different faiths should not join in a business of this kind if all show moderation and good will. Best of all this to you, I feel sure," he said to the Brents, "will be to know that we will have with us on the *Ark* and the *Dove* two Jesuit priests— Father White and Father Altham—and two lay brothers. Not only do they go to preach the Gospel to the Indians, but we will have in Maryland what we enjoy here so rarely: the ministrations of priests of our own religion."

At this news Margaret turned her eyes toward the fire, for

suddenly they seemed to be full of tears.

All were gathered around the hearth, Margaret and Mary seated together on a chimney seat, the gentlemen standing before the blazing logs.

"This is the way of it, Leonard," Fulke was saying. "Definitely you can count on Giles and me to send out at the very least ten servants.

But until things are more settled here, until our mother's health improves and our father is in better spirits, I believe it would be faithless and cruel to both for any of us to go out to Maryland with you this year."

Giles was pursing his lips with a little frustration, and shifting his weight from one foot to the other.

"Mind you," he said quickly, "we are enthusiastic and we will come in time, as soon a time as may be. Meanwhile . . ."

"Meanwhile," Margaret picked up the word, "Mary and I have just decided we, too, will send some servants. We agreed on five, didn't we, sister?" she added, looking at Mary, and reaching for one of her hands she squeezed it tightly.

But Mary was not cooperative.

"When did we reach such a decision? "

"Oh," said Margaret, "you are such a tease, Mary. Why, not ten minutes ago."

"But I had hoped—" Leonard began, and then stopped suddenly, his face flushing.

"I know," Margaret told him, "but Fulke has explained everything to you very thoroughly. You must realize at this time we cannot leave our parents—"

"—in this 'miserable little hut,' " finished Giles, smiling broadly. " 'Pon my soul, Leonard, you cannot comprehend how badly our sire has taken this move. It is all he speaks of—Larke Stoke, his 'miserable little hut.' "

But Giles saw that Leonard was barely listening. He was looking at Margaret, a deep, keen disappointment in his eyes. Winking slyly at Fulke, Giles said, "If you will excuse us, we have a habit at this hour of visiting our father. We will be only a half-hour, but he requires punctuality. Mary, if you wish to join us I'll ask Tidd to get your shawl."

"Mary has a cold and cannot be in Papa's chilly room," Margaret said quickly.

"On the contrary," contradicted Mary, "that was last week if you recall. I am completely free of the affliction and I know Papa would be pleased to have me join him." Margaret's shoulders slumped. How could Mary fail her at this moment?

When they had gone Leonard, appreciating Margaret's confusion, said casually, "By the bye, if you and Mary will send servants out with us, you must sign this list of Adventurers—that is sign for the five servants."

And he took from his waistcoat pocket a long scroll. Unrolling it, he flattened it out on the table by the window where there were quill and ink and sand shaker.

Uneasily Margaret picked up the quill. "Where shall I sign? " she asked in a low voice.

"Right here, just under Giles's signature."

Margaret read the signature aloud, "Giles Brent, Gentleman Adventurer. Um!" she muttered. "Very well, as you will."

Slowly, with fine flourishes and shadings, she inscribed her name, "Margaret Brent, Gent. Adventurer."

"Zounds!" exclaimed Leonard, a merry glint in his eye. "Cecilius will find this amusingly irregular."

"Lady Adventurer would be most objectionable and misleading," Margaret told him.

As she put down the sand shaker which she had used to

blot her signature, Leonard reached for her hand. She did not pull away, but looked into his eyes seriously.

"You will not come with me, Margaret?" he asked pleadingly.

"Think you I could, in the face of circumstances as Fulke has stated them?"

Leonard sighed heavily. His eyes fell to the scroll and seeing that the ink was dry he began to roll it up slowly.

"And does this mean—"

"Leonard!" Margaret interrupted. "You are going on a long voyage, a voyage full of peril. Let our parting be as it has always been—kinsman to kinsman—warm, friendly, affectionate. I know you deserve more; more I cannot give now. Always I have been fond of you, always, but what you wish me to say requires more than fondness, Leonard. You would wish me to admit this. It cannot be too long before some of us will follow you to Maryland. We have talked of it much, though I shall have a time to persuade Mary."

There was an awkward pause. Leonard made no move to speak. His disappointment was crushing. Margaret realized this, and her heart ached. He had asked her so often, and so often she had eased him with excuses. She did not have the courage boldly and frankly to say she did not love him enough to marry him, nor to insist upon the point she was six years his senior. That fact, of itself, would count against their marriage, at least in her mind.

Now she spoke truthfully, not intending to give him the hope he inwardly grasped from her words. "Not a day shall pass when you leave but I will think of you, Leonard, pray for you and the success of the Maryland venture. And I shall be impatient with each day's delay of our following you. What more can I say now?"

*The* Ark *and the* Dove *sail off for the New World*

"Just one more word," Leonard replied frankly.

"No, Leonard."

Margaret meant not another word at the moment, but Leonard took the "No" more seriously. It seemed to startle him momentarily. Then, standing erect and managing a sad smile, he put his hands on her shoulders and kissed her tenderly on each cheek.

Six months later, in command of the *Ark* and the *Dove* expedition, he sailed from Cowes on the Isle of Wight for Maryland. It was St. Cecilia's day, 1633. It would be five years before he saw Margaret again.

# 3.

# Daydreams and Sorrows

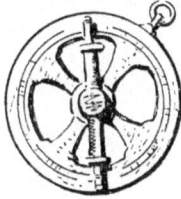

MARY said the *Ark* and the *Dove* could run into bad storms; they could even be wrecked. But Margaret refused to think such thoughts. In her mind the Maryland colony was going to be a wonderful reality. And there, in the New World, she and Mary would own one thousand acres of free land. Over and over, day and night, she found herself wishing it had been possible for Fulke, Giles, Mary, and herself to have gone with Leonard on the *Ark*.

The Lord Baltimore, Cecilius Calvert, gave every "gentleman adventurer" two hundred acres of land for each indentured servant taken or sent to Maryland: and Margaret and Mary had sent five. Indentured servants were persons from every and any walk of life anxious to settle in the New World but unable to pay their passage over the ocean. In exchange for this payment by another person, the servant agreed to work for him for four years. At the end of that time the one who paid his passage agreed to give him fifty acres of land, some agricultural tools, some corn and wheat and a new suit of clothes. Then the servant was a free man. He could start his own plantation, follow his trade or profession—for some were carpenters, others farmers, others lawyers or even doctors—have a vote in the affairs of the colony, and in every way be on an equal footing with the other free men.

Fulke and Giles had sent twenty servants on the *Ark* so they each had two thousand acres, quite enough to start extensive tobacco plantations; and tobacco, shipped to

England, brought a handsome price. They anticipated, once their first crop was sold, that they would be able to ease the considerable financial burdens of their father, Sir Richard. And they were not disappointed. They dreamed that in a few years they might have enough to buy back for him his land and his former home, Admington Manor.

The very idea of buying back what was rightfully his almost gave Sir Richard a fatal stroke.

He alternately stormed and brooded over his lot, but once his sons were able to pay his monthly fines for him and deposit reserves in his account he began to feel better. The first indication of this was his stubbornness. He would wait, he said, until the Crown returned to him his confiscated property. Not one pound would he pay to buy it back.

It was not until the late summer of 1634 that Margaret had a letter from Leonard telling of their safe arrival after a dreadful voyage during which the *Ark* lost the *Dove* for a full six weeks. They had landed in March and at once, said Leonard, they had erected a great cross and Father White, the head of the Jesuit mission to Maryland, had offered a Mass of thanksgiving. Meanwhile the Protestants held their own religious service. He told of buying the site of St. Mary's City from friendly Indians who had been planning to move anyway. The transaction was accomplished with the aid of an Englishman by the name of Henry Fleete, who had lived among the Indians for twenty years and spoke their language fluently.

Leonard mentioned a William Claiborne, too, as the only seemingly hostile person so far met. Claiborne had a prosperous trading post with the Indians on an island called Kent in the Chesapeake Bay about sixty miles north of St. Mary's City. He enclosed a rough map for them all to study so they could see the lay of the land.

He ended his letter on a personal note, telling Margaret that for his part he was still of the same mind as he had always been, that he was waiting as patiently as could be for the four Brents to come to Maryland—but most especially for Margaret herself.

Margaret frowned and fretted over this ending.

"Will he never understand my answer is 'No'?" she complained to Mary. "The time is going to come when I am going to have to hurt Leonard deeply—if only he would understand and not make this necessary."

"I'm sorry you feel as you do," Mary told her. "Leonard would make a fine brother-in-law. But it's a greater shame that he is so dull he does not understand you. Leonard should marry. He needs a wife. Every man does."

"Agreed for the sake of peace," Margaret answered. "But he does not need me. I am too old. Brides are chits of girls in their teens. Fancy me a bride with a veil and a long train at my age!"

"The veil and the dress do not make the bride," Mary told her, "but—"

"But, Mary," Margaret took her up, "I, we, all of us, have known such trouble that I find my heart, for one, has hatched such a yearning for freedom and independence, even for adventure, that never shall I have the least desire to marry anyone, ever."

"Trouble is you cannot see marriage as an adventure."

"As a shackle, Mary. Not to be free to do this or that but by m'lord's leave? Ah! No. Not for me."

"Well, I crave freedom and independence, too," said Mary, "but I'd like safety and security with it, and someone to worry things through with me. I have no yearning for adventure, as you call it, though. That is too uncertain. Adventure! Margaret, 'tis a man who seeks adventure, not a woman. Must be your red hair has hatched that notion for you."

Mary's eyes were laughing as she said this teasingly. But Margaret didn't think it was funny.

"It's in my blood," she retorted quickly, "and you have it, too. Once you felt the deck of a ship under your two feet—a ship bound for Maryland—you'd feel it, too."

"I'd feel nothing but the most fearful and disagreeable attack of *mal de mer*," said Mary firmly, "and don't you forget that."

In the following months that ran into years, Leonard sent many more letters to Larke Stoke detailing the progress of the small colony, and always mentioning the great spiritual release all felt to be able openly to practice their religion.

He often spoke of Father White. "He begs and pleads with us to let him start his mission among the Indians," he said, "but the Council and I think it not yet safe for him to go among them alone, and with a protective company the natives would suspect hostility and the purpose of the mission would be thwarted. Father Altham agrees with us but fails to impress his superior with the wisdom of our decision. Father White is in his late fifties and fears he may be taken before this great mission of his life is even begun."

In another letter he wrote, "As yet no Protestant minister has come among us, though in number we are here more Protestant than Catholic, and we have set aside in our treasury a sum of 500 pounds of tobacco against the salary of such an one when he may come to Maryland. Meanwhile, we are building a chapel of native brick, much to the edification of Father White, and all of us for that matter. When complete, the Protestants will also be free to use it for what services they may devise if they wish."

Every letter from Leonard reaching Larke Stoke was eagerly read and reread, and merely increased the Brents' impatience to be off to Maryland themselves. But Lady Elizabeth was in such frail health now that no one would think of causing such a great upheaval in the family circle.

Meanwhile Giles sent instructions to his servants to build him a fine house against the day when he would surely be able to settle there. Not to be outdone, Margaret spent days and weeks dreaming up a dream house for Mary and herself, drawing one plan then another.

"Do you mean to say when we do get to Maryland we shan't live with Giles?" Mary asked her when the idea first fired Margaret's imagination.

"Would that be freedom?" Margaret challenged in reply. "How long do you think that would last? Mark my words, Giles will take a wife. Shall his sisters then be welcome? Be practical, Mary. We are spinsters and remaining so. We must have our own domicile from the start."

The "start," as it developed, was sad. Lady Elizabeth died in September, 1637. She had never been really well since the birth of Ann ten years previously.

With the exception of Jane, the six daughters were at home when their mother died. Also Lady Elizabeth's sons Fulke, Giles, William, and George—the other two, as well as Jane, were married.

It was about ten days after the funeral that Sir Richard called these sons and daughters together in the drawing room at Larke Stoke. He was in a gentle, mellow mood, saddened by the loss of his wife, thoughtful and quiet as they all gathered. It was evening. The curtains were drawn against the chill of the September night and a low fire burned on the hearth.

*Sir Richard smiled at them, his eyes misting a little*

Sir Richard looked about him at the faces of his children as though mentally calling the role. He smiled at them, his eyes misting a little. Then with a deep sigh he spoke to them all.

"The time has come for those of you who wish to go your separate ways to go. Your mother no longer has need of you, and I—I am not of a mind to tie you to my remaining years. Well I know there are those of you who wish to go out to the colonies. Go, my children, with my blessing. Fulke, you have Maryland in your blood, I know. Go, while yet I live. Try your fortune. There will be time enough for you to live in England when you inherit my title and property—what has been left me of the latter. William will stay with me; he wishes it so."

"Oh, Papa," Margaret took advantage of a pause, "you are so generous, so good to us all—you make it possible yet difficult for us to follow our selfish desires."

"Not at all," put in Elizabeth, who for many years had supplanted her mother as active head of her father's household. "We all have planned it among ourselves. Ann, our sweet little sister, of course will stay here with me, and Catherine and Eleanor, too. With William we will make a merry home for Papa. It is only right that those of you who have wanted other lives should have them now."

"Elizabeth is right," said Sir Richard. "Wherever your paths lead, my children, know you have my blessing, that I expect you to give an account of yourselves, wherever you be, worthy, of our heritage. And remember, too, your father will never forget your devotion and faithfulness these past few years, especially during your mother's long illness. You are my greatest wealth, all of you my most precious jewels which the Crown of England can never snatch from me. Now go your ways in peace; make your own lives. I send you with my love, my tender, lasting love."

The Brents would recall no more solemn moment in their lives than this; and for them all it was a strangely happy one, too. Now Fulke, Giles, Margaret, and Mary were free at last to go to Maryland, to begin their great adventure.

But it took them almost a year to get ready. And this was because, first, the pace of living in the seventeenth century was like the slow drip of a faucet that needs a new washer. Second, packing to go to Maryland was not merely a matter of putting their clothes in their trunks. There would be a great deal more than clothes to take. Almost everything they would need in their new homes, both indoors and outdoors, had to be purchased, packed, labeled, carted to dockside over the rough country roads and stowed away on board ship. It took a great deal of careful thinking, planning, checking and rechecking dozens of lists and memoranda.

They had to take nails, hinges, latches, locks and bolts for their houses; andirons, waffle irons, kettles, pots, spiders, trivets, pewter; bedding, furniture, carpets, linens, curtain and dress materials; horses, cows, sheep, chickens, dogs; plows, harrows, shovels, hoes, axes, rakes; and last, for the voyage itself, they had to provide their own beds and bedding, their food and cooking utensils.

Each day of preparation brought closer the day of parting. Even Giles, always in something of a bluster, quite a man of the world, became more and more subdued as the summer of 1638 wore on and their day of sailing grew nearer. Margaret and Mary were quiet as mice, keeping their thoughts and emotions to themselves, noticing every least detail about Larke Stoke more keenly than ever before, as though to impress a complete memory in their hearts. For them, this great adventure would be "until death"; they never expected to return to England. Unhappy as had been their life in Glouchestershire, it was not without heavy hearts that they came to the dawn of the day of farewells.

Parting with Sir Richard, whom they realized they'd never see again in this life, was heartbreaking. And Margaret found saying good-by to little Ann harder than to any of the others. Ann had been her special care since Sir Richard had had to dismiss her governess. Margaret begged her father to let her take Ann with them to Maryland. But he was adamant in his refusal. Ann, he said, when she came of age would make her own choice, as he had given all the others leave to do.

When she was at sea, Margaret was misty-eyed for many days and by night shed tears of homesickness and heartache. She marveled that something she wanted so much, something she had waited for so long, could now cost so dearly in pain and sorrow.

# 4.

# Maryland . . . and an Answer

THE Brents took ship at the great port of Bristol on the Severn River. They started at a time of year when, inevitably, they ran into the usual equinoctial storms over the Atlantic, and hurricane gales and resulting high seas made a rough voyage.

True to her predictions, Mary was miserably seasick. Nothing could relieve her distress but the impossible—the calming of the stormy seas. The ship rolled and pitched night and day incessantly, and she lay on her bed in the airless cabin, unable to take food, and surrounded by other ladies with the same affliction. Margaret soon put her emotional misery out of her mind to watch beside Mary and comfort her as best she could.

The storms delayed them for many weeks, but at long last, on the feast of St. Cecilia, November 22, 1638, they docked at St. Mary's City in Maryland.

On the whole, Margaret and her brothers had been good sailors, and arrived in good health and high spirits. But Mary was pitiful, she looked so pale and haggard. Fulke and Giles made a chair for her with their hands and carried her ashore. Here Leonard and a host of the prominent people of the colony waited to greet the Brents warmly.

Among them was Father White, who had delayed the hour of the morning Mass until they landed, believing they would cherish the memory of their first moments in Maryland spent in the Chapel assisting at the Holy Sacrifice. The very thought of this had a wonderful effect upon Mary. She brightened noticeably and insisted she was well enough to go to the Chapel. Margaret had been of a mind to put her to bed right away. But Mary said, no indeed.

Leonard had thoughtfully provided horses for them, even including one for Tidd, Sir Richard's old servant. At his master's request, he had come out to Maryland willingly enough to serve in the sisters' household.

It was a memorable occasion! For the first time in their lives the Brents could enter a Catholic chapel, openly hear Mass and receive Holy Communion without fear of fine or prison.

The Chapel had been dedicated the previous Christmas Day. It was built of native brick, measured 18 by 30 feet, a "cathedral" in the wilderness. It stood at the northwest corner of Middle and Mattapany Streets. A servant of Captain Cornwayles', styling himself an artist, had painted a mural back of the altar which had a lot of red in it. The Brents learned later it was to represent the flames of Pentecost. That morning they found it very distracting.

Following this solemn occasion of thanksgiving, Leonard provided a breakfast at St. Gabriel's, the name of his residence. It was more like a banquet than a mere breakfast. The great oblong mahogany council table in the hall was covered with a fine white linen cloth from Ireland and then truly loaded with good things to eat. There were smoked hams, fried chicken, fresh oysters and salt mackerel, corn puddings, waffles, English crumpets, jams and jellies, stewed apples and plums, mounds of fresh-churned butter, beakers of rich, golden creamy milk. There was no coffee; the hot morning beverage was a "tea" brewed from the dried leaves of the wild raspberry or the yaupon, a kind of holly.

Bit by bit, in the warm hospitality of the Maryland welcome, Mary regained her spirits and animation. As the breakfast continued she managed to eat, sparsely but with confidence— something she had not done for weeks.

Father White was the star guest, so to say. His pink-cheeked face radiated happiness. There was a new hope in his eyes as he made a special point of speaking confidentially with Giles.

"Leonard tells me you will be one of the Council, and Treasurer of the Colony as well. This is splendid, my son, as it means you will have a voice in our affairs. And I am quick to take advantage of your big heart to implore you to use your influence with the Council to secure from them permission for me to go among the Piscataways. Five years I have waited to begin my mission to the natives. Not yet am I permitted to do so."

"But with good reason, Father? Is this not so?" Giles answered, beaming with pleasure, flattered by Father White's direct appeal. "If it be not safe," he went on gently, "I could not urge what you wish. You are too precious to the Maryland venture. Think, for instance, how far my brother and sisters and I have come, and at what pain to the heart, in order to have your ministrations. Think you your order can spare priests to us merely to be killed by the Indians?"

"But they are friendly," insisted Father White. "And think of the souls to be brought to Our Lord. Only a short distance to the north of us here lives the Emperor of the Piscataways in their capital village of Kittamaquaandi. He is chief of practically all the extent of my Lord Baltimore's patent. Oh, but to be allowed to go to them. Keep in mind, my son, I am no longer young."

Captain Cornwayles joined them. He was the wealthiest

settler, a man of great military experience, a true diplomat, and had been a Councillor since the beginning of the colony. He shook his head smilingly at Father White as he said to Giles, "Well I know what our good friend has put to you. Do not let his zeal set your own afire until you hear our views."

"It is one good thing to be prudent," Father White replied, "and one sad, even evil thing to be imprudent."

"Come, now, Father," remonstrated the Captain gently, "not before our friend Captain Brent, and him with his feet barely steadied on the ground. Give him a bit of time. We are all with you, Father, you must know that. But this occasion is to welcome our newcomers before we tell them our troubles."

"Ah, troubles," returned Giles. "Would it be life to be wholly free of them?" He smiled. "Come," he said, "I see Leonard conferring with my brother Fulke. Shall we join them?"

"And your sisters? " asked the Captain. "They are yonder, as you may see, womanlike, chatting away with some of the ladies."

And so they were. Margaret and Mary did their best to listen attentively to those who surrounded them. But it seemed that everyone talked at once and it was difficult to give ear to everything that was said.

Next to Mary sat Eleanor Hawley, widow of Jerome Hawley who had come out with Leonard as a member of the Council and Secretary of the Colony. She had a wee house close by the Chapel and was telling Mary, ". . . take full charge of everything, dear. The linens and vestments and the altar—flowers—so difficult in winter. And I keep it clean, too. Father has been good to let me do this. Perhaps you will like to share the privilege with me."

Anne Lewger was next to Margaret. Her husband John was now the Secretary and an important member of the

Council. He had been a classmate of Cecilius Calvert, the Lord Baltimore, at Oxford University, and was his close friend.

Speaking behind her hand, Anne Lewger was saying to Margaret, "Don't take Mrs. Neale too seriously. She is quite charming, really, but before she and her husband James came out here she had been lady in waiting to our Queen, and she seems unable to forget it. Now and then she'll be a bit uppity but she has a heart of gold and is a wonderful hostess. We have lovely parties at the Neales' during our dull winter months which are beginning now. You'll see."

It was Leonard who interrupted the buzzing about Margaret and Mary.

"I had planned, if it met with your pleasure," he told them, "to take you about our city. It will not take us long, for we are not yet of extensive proportions."

It didn't take very long at all.

They started down Middle Street toward the water front, and the old Mulberry Tree on which were posted all public notices. The old tree was the "newspaper center of the city," except for the fact that it towered over the bluff overlooking St. Mary's Bay. Turning left from here they followed St. George's River past the site of the Council Chambers, not yet built, and Smith's Towne House to the Fort. The Fort was the first construction undertaken by the 1633 arrivals. Here the party turned left again, north of the Fort, to the site of the Governor's Castle. Workmen were beginning to clear the ground for the building which would be started as soon as spring and the New Year of 1639 came, in about four month's time.

After Leonard had explained the plans for this castle, he turned his horse about again and led them all to Giles's beautiful White House, across Key's Branch, south of the Fort.

"Here is your castle," Leonard told Giles, "the envy of many. Your servants have done a fine piece of work."

Giles reined in his horse and sat in the saddle gazing about him with evident pride and satisfaction.

"Who named it 'The White House'?" he asked Leonard.

"Why, the name just fell to it naturally. Look at that wonderful exterior. A fine plaster we make here of our crushed oyster shells."

"For bachelor quarters, not bad, eh, Fulke?" said Giles, turning to his brother.

"I hope to goodness no one has named our house," put in Margaret.

"No, indeed," added Mary, "we're calling ours the Sisters' Freehold and any other name will not stand."

"I say," put in Fulke, speaking to Giles, "you have a handsome structure there. I wonder —is it weathertight? "

"Should be," Giles told him, "I instructed that it be insulated with seaweed and plastered inside as well. That should keep the weather out."

"Leonard, what's the matter?" Margaret broke in. "You look—well, somewhat distressed."

"I am puzzled," admitted Leonard.

"Over what?" asked Margaret.

"Over what Mary just said. Surely you girls are not going to live alone?"

"But surely we are," said Mary.

"Oh, yes, definitely," said Fulke. "They have been planning this—"

"Come," interrupted Giles in a tone of command, realizing this trend of chatter would lead to further surprise for Leonard. "Let's get inside my fine house. See the smoke from that chimney yonder? It tells me there's a fine, roaring fire waiting for us."

"Hold a minute," protested Margaret. "May we not just see our house first, Giles, please?"

"Your house?" asked Leonard, his brow crinkled in a frown and his eyes incredulous. "You must be mistaken."

"Something must be very wrong," Margaret said apprehensively. "Please, Leonard, show Mary and me our town land and our—"

"Yes, by all means, let us find out immediately," said Leonard, turning his horse. "Just follow me. I am very much afraid there has been a great mistake."

Giles's tract of town land comprised sixty acres along the river. They followed the river now, and soon came abreast of Smith's forge, built and owned by a former indentured servant of Fulke to whom Giles had deeded some land at the southern end of his tract. Next they came upon the seventy-acre tract owned by Margaret and Mary within the limits of St. Mary's City.

There was very little conversation as the four Brents followed Leonard. Presently he stopped and, turning his horse to face inshore, silently looked at the Brent sisters.

"This must be your tract," said Fulke.

"Nice slope to the land," added Giles. "You'll have good drainage."

"But where is our house?" asked Mary, dismayed, for there was only one building in sight—a small box-like hut with a steep roof and one chimney.

"Whoever put that there," said Giles, "should have had it removed before we arrived."

"But your servants built it," said Leonard.

"Our servants?" asked Margaret, horrified. "Impossible."

"You mean to say . . ."

*"Papa should see this miserable little hut"*

"We sent the most wonderful plans," Margaret told him, her voice quivering. "What can have gone wrong?"

"That will have to come down right away," said Fulke. "And you girls will have to accept the hospitality of Giles and myself. And I, personally, will punish the servants who have done this to you—"

"But wait," Leonard cut in, completely confused about the whole thing. "Those servants are free now. Don't you recall their term of indenture expired this fall?"

"This is simply dreadful," said Margaret. "For five years we have been looking forward . . . Oh, Papa should see *this* miserable little hut. I'd not even house our horses or our spaniels in that horrid . . ."

"But I had no idea you planned to live alone," Leonard said. "This you should have told me. Because it cannot be allowed for more than . . ."

Giles and Fulke had drawn alongside their sisters.

"I am sorry as I can be," Giles told Margaret, while Fulke comforted Mary. Giles reached his hand to Margaret's shoulder. "This is a cruel disappointment, sister," he said gently. "You let me handle it. I will see that those who were your servants make restitution in time and labor to follow the plans you and Mary have drawn. And come, admit, even though you have to be my guests, it will be a thrill to be here on the spot to watch each plank and nail as your dream house comes to life."

For a moment Margaret rested her cheek on Giles's hand. "You do understand, don't you?" she said, looking at him through eyes swimming with unshed tears. "I am so disappointed I could crawl in the woods yonder and wail my heart out."

Leonard drew near.

"I am sorry, too, Margaret," he said softly, "but you can't know the hope I have, realizing now you intend to live alone, for I know it means . . ."

"Don't, Leonard, don't." Margaret cut him short. "Presently I will explain. But it does not mean what you think it does. Mary and I have a piece of writing from Cecilius."

"This I must hear," said Leonard. Then, turning in his saddle, he asked the others, "Will you all forgive us if Margaret and I ride on ahead a bit?"

"Trot along," said Fulke lightly, "we'll bring up the rear at a discreet distance."

When they were out of earshot, Leonard slowed his horse and Margaret drew in hers to keep pace.

"The day is not half done," said Leonard, "yet 'pon my soul it is to this point the longest of my life. I've been waiting, waiting, Margaret, to have your ear alone, to say how happy beyond words I am that you have come. To say, my Margaret, I still love you, I . ."

"Oh, Leonard," Margaret pleaded. "Not now, I beg you. It has been a long day, as you say. So full of new sights, new people, new emotions as to confound me completely. Then to have it spoiled, you might say, by that horrible little shanty! Whatever shall we do? Mary and I have brought furniture and furnishings for a six-room house as we planned. Wherever shall we store it all until we do have our home? I am heartsick, Leonard, so . . . Oh, but I'm selfish, too. What a wonderful welcome you have given us: and it is so good to see you, too. Forgive me for thinking only of the trouble."

"Trouble," mused Leonard, a trace of bitterness in his tone as though his thoughts had double meaning. He urged his horse on a little faster. "The piece of writing you mentioned from Cecilius—what is it?"

"We knew of the law," Margaret began to explain.

"The law?"

"Yes, you know, about spinsters here. The law that a woman cannot hold property in her own name for more than seven years. By that time she must either marry or give it up."

"Continue," Leonard prompted her.

"Ridiculous law, isn't it? " Margaret dallied.

"It was Father Altham who proposed it to us," Leonard told her. "He persuaded Cecilius that no woman here vow chastity in the world. In the wilderness, Margaret, there must be an able-bodied man in every household. At any time any house among us may have to become a fort."

"Yes, we know. Cecilius told us all about it. He came to Larke Stoke to visit us after Mama's death. It was good of him. But when he told us of this law concerning spinster settlers, I asked him as a special favor to make an exception of Mary and myself. And bless his soul, he did just that. I have his order in my reticule."

Leonard said nothing for a long time. They rode on silently. Soon Giles's house came into view, and presently they turned their horses into the wide oyster-shell driveway leading from Giles's private wharf to his house.

"I see it all now," Leonard finally said, not looking at Margaret. His eyes were straight ahead and his chin high, though the tone of his voice was very sorrowful. "That you have taken such pains to circumvent this law dashes all my hopes. Oh, Margaret! This is cruel."

"It is dreadful," agreed Margaret, "after the wonderful welcome you have given us, to have this come out in the open now. I had thought in a week or so . . . But it is your fault, Leonard. You have pressed the point because Mary and I are planning to live alone."

Leonard didn't say a word, and Margaret felt uneasy.

"You should have expected this, truly," she finally said, "for often, if you will reflect, I have tried to tell you as much, but not in a way to hurt you. I love you very much, Leonard, and I always shall, but I do not love you as a wife should."

Leonard turned quickly to search Margaret's eyes, his own hurt and pleading. Then as quickly he looked away. His shoulders slumped and his cheeks flushed. To Margaret he seemed to shrink in the saddle. She felt a great compassion for him. Comforting words of endearment flew through her mind but she dared not utter them for, manlike, from them he would take renewed hope rather than consolation.

"I wish we had thought of this all when I was seventeen—but then, how could we, for you were only eleven? Don't you see, Leonard? You must have a young, vivacious bride, not an older woman, set in her ways, and with the best half of her life behind her."

"The best half?" repeated Leonard absently. "Youth is the best half of any life, isn't it?" She saw the muscles in Leonard's face twitch. His cheeks were pale now, and a deep frown dented his forehead.

"I will never be able to think of you as old, Margaret. Age is not a counting of years; it is an idea. I am sorry," he added bitterly, "you've got hold of it." He flushed again with that bitter barb, but he did not take it back, did not say he was sorry. His disappointment was crushing his heart as he said, "At least it is a consolation that you are in Maryland where I shall be able to see you, talk with you, and . . ."

"That's right, Leonard," Margaret put in quickly, "and I hope you will spend much time at the Freehold when at last we have it."

# 5

# Homebuilding, and an Enemy

IN THE weeks that followed the memorable day of their arrival Margaret and Mary had so many things to occupy their waking hours and their thoughts after they'd gone to bed at night.

First of all, now that they had seen the houses others had built here, (most of them were called "manors") and especially Giles's fine White House, Margaret drastically revised their plans for the Freehold.

This name which they had chosen for their residence in St. Mary's City was not a fantastic whim. In 1636 the Lord Baltimore had revised his original "Conditions of Plantation." He wanted to make them more attractive so that many more settlers would go to Maryland. So, he provided that everyone who had 3,000 or more acres might enjoy the privileges of "Court Baron and Court Leet." This meant that the owners of such large plantations would have private jurisdiction and dispense justice among any of their servants who might get into trouble among themselves or commit serious crimes— theft, or perhaps murder. In the same document, though, the Lord Baltimore said there might also be "freeholds." The owners of freeholds, no matter how much land they had, would not be responsible for dispensing justice. Any disputes or crimes among their servants could be settled in the provincial court.

As a matter of fact, ever since 1633 Margaret and Mary had kept sending servants out to Maryland on almost every ship; when they themselves finally arrived they had almost

6,000 acres of land, for they had sent nearly thirty servants. So Margaret and Mary could have held Court Baron and Court Leet, having their servants swear fealty to them and acting as judges over all disputes. But they had no wish to go in for all this and wanted no part of it. Margaret said if they called their "manor" the Sisters' Freehold there would be no mistake about their rejection of all the fussy court business. And Mary said, too, the name, the Sisters' Freehold, would have a double meaning because of the special exception the Lord Baltimore had made for them. They could hold their home freely forever; they would not have to give it up in seven years—or marry to keep it.

When Margaret showed her final drawings to Mary, asking her approval of the revised plans, Mary looked at her wide-eyed.

"Gracious mercy me!" she exclaimed. "Brick and iron grilles, two—maybe three, stories? Are you feeling quite right, Margaret, dear? Six bedrooms? Whoever heard of such a mansion for two spinsters? Now, Margaret, this won't do. It won't do at all. It's all much too pretentious."

"How can you say that?" Margaret asked her, in a half-hurt, half-coaxing tone. "Can this be too pretentious for the sisters of Giles Brent?"

Mary looked at her, giving in as she always did to Margaret.

"So," she said, "you'd not for the life of you live with Giles, run his home, be his hostess; but you want to live up to him, eh? Even beyond him? Oh, my Margaret, you're such a true woman!"

"Our brother is to be a person of great importance and substance," Margaret defended her new "dream-house" plans, "and it would never do for us to be a humiliation to him with a—" she paused, smiling a little sadly—"with a 'miserable little hut'—now would it?"

"Tell me just one thing," Mary said, being practical, "how are we going to pay for this castle on the river? "

"Why, out of our first year's tobacco crop, how else?" Margaret replied, implying it was unnecessary to bother to ask that question.

"It's going to be very expensive," Mary added, "and lovely when it is finished. I hope it won't take too long to build it."

While they were absorbed with progress on the Freehold, and by every ship Margaret sent orders abroad for special materials, Giles was busy, too, building another home for himself on the Island of Kent which he called Kent Fort Manor. Leonard had decided to make Giles the Commander of Kent, feeling he would be just the one to suppress the arrogant William Claiborne who was causing constant friction and trouble there.

Then, before Margaret and Mary realized it, Christmas was almost upon them—their first in Maryland. It was a memorable one for the gifts and festivities, the parties, the beautiful Christmas Mass in the Chapel.

Christmas night was the first opportunity Leonard could find to go over the Claiborne affair in detail with Giles and Margaret. Mary was welcome to hear about it, too, but she chose to spend the night with Eleanor Hawley who was experiencing the first Christmas of her widowhood and feeling very depressed.

Leonard told Giles, "It is of vital importance that you know every detail from the beginning. I have a mountain of documents here which I am going to leave with you so you can study them carefully. I hope you will do this before you return to Kent. As you know, my cousin William Brainthwaite is already Governor, but," he went on tersely, "we find the Governor is an authority Claiborne chooses to ignore."

"Let him ignore me to his sorrow," said Giles.

"See that you are very careful, Giles," Margaret said. "I gather the man might not stop at an ambush, assassination."

"You ladies always get so alarmed," returned Giles.

"Now hear me, both of you," Leonard cut in. "Cecilius, who cannot have the faintest idea of how troublesome the scoundrel is, keeps writing me to treat him amicably. That's the rub! Cecilius will not understand that Claiborne has no wish to be amicable. He doesn't even know what that means."

"But why? " asked Margaret, puzzled.

"Don't you know," came Fulke's voice from a corner of the room where he was keeping more or less aloof, reading the recent letters from Larke Stoke over again, "that some are born into the world just plain ornery?"

Leonard ignored the remark.

"Handicapped as we are by Cecilius's long-range views," he went on, "I charge you, Giles, to put the villain in his place and keep him there. It will take a lot of clever ingenuity."

"Where is his place?" asked Margaret.

Giles looked at her a trifle impatiently.

"Margaret," he said quietly, "it is I who am to handle this matter."

"Don't be cross," Margaret begged.

"His place is in Virginia," Leonard said, smiling at the little interchange between Giles and Margaret. Then his expression became grave once more.

"Let me say here," he resumed crisply, "there will not be use nor need for you to try to handle Claiborne with velvet gloves. At the direction of Cecilius, nay, even His Majesty, we've been all over that. It won't work. Claiborne is a scheming scoundrel. He would dissipate and ruin the Colony. He has most of Virginia behind him. He has stirred the people against us—holding over them the dire threat of the proximity of 'Papists'—to which he personally is quite indifferent. This is merely a handy cover for his greed. He understands only one language—gunfire. But, mark you, on those occasions when it has come to this, the blackguard has managed to be well out of range. He leaves his hirelings to take our shot, to spill their blood, to die of their wounds."

"Go on," said Giles, pressing his lips together into a thin, hard line.

"We have to admit that when Cecilius received the charter for Maryland, Claiborne was well entrenched on Kent; had been since 1621. He had a good trade with the Indians. He was wealthy. He carried prestige and influence in Virginia. He is Surveyor of the Province, Secretary of State—his voice is powerful in the ear of His Majesty. And, as you can see by this," Leonard went on, unrolling one of the papers and handing it to Giles, "he received His Majesty's blessing on his trade with the natives."

Giles reached for the candelabrum, pulling it nearer to him as he studied the document carefully.

Presently he looked up at Leonard.

"Of all the . . ."

"Exactly," said Leonard. "Now, although he never received a grant of land, Claiborne claims this document is a bona-fide title to Kent and that on the strength of it he bought the Island from the Indians on the thirteenth of August, 1631. Then, as you recall, in 1632 Cecilius, twentieth of June, received the charter for Maryland. From that moment forward Claiborne has thrown fat into the fire. No sooner had we landed here than he wrote personally to His Majesty suggesting that the

*"The lying, whining old sniveler," said Giles.*

Lord Baltimore could settle in some other place . . . you'll find that neat idea in this document."

"How have you got hold of all these personal papers of Claiborne's?" asked Margaret.

"Yes," added Giles, "that's a good question. How have you?"

"By confiscation, along with all his belongings found on Kent, including his cattle and his servants."

"So that's what the fellow means in this letter to the King about 'tumults and fighting and bloodshed.' "

Leonard nodded.

"You may depend on Claiborne to be out of the way when there's blood being shed," he said. "Two of his men were killed in the attack, but he himself fled to the sanctuary of Virginia."

"And he has the gall to write the King here that the Marylanders are disobeying all commands to be peaceable and conciliatory. Oh, that rotten, lying, whining old sniveler," said Giles.

"Agreed," said Leonard. "But to get on with this. Governor Harvey of Virginia is our friend—would do anything in his power for us—but Claiborne has the rank and file of the Virginians so dead set against us that Harvey stands alone. Even on his own Council."

"As you get through these documents," Leonard concluded, "you'll see right and justice are on our side by this order from the Lords of Plantation given from Whitehall on the fourth of April last, to wit, that Kent is beyond dispute within Cecilius's patent and all right and title to it rest with him."

"Has a copy of this been registered with Claiborne?" asked Giles.

"This is his copy, remember? These are confiscated documents. But Claiborne claims this one to be a forgery."

"I'll change his mind for him on that point," Giles promised.

# 6

# A Baptism and a Bride to Be

BY THE fall of 1639 Margaret and Mary were settled comfortably in the Freehold, and at Margaret's special urging, Giles came down from Kent to visit them.

When he saw their new home he was appalled at its size, but very proud. "It's big enough," he told his sisters, "to house a whole community of holy nuns, which you, my dears, are not."

But he was generous with his praise and admiration. He liked the large casement windows, the great fireplaces in every room, the fan pattern of the brick over the windows and doorways.

And then he said, standing off from the house down the driveway, "What happened about the roof?"

For all her figuring and measuring, Margaret had not ordered enough red tile from Spain, so part of the roof was of slate.

"You should have had me figure that out for you," Giles told her sternly.

Margaret accepted the comment meekly.

"Now come inside," she urged.

"I say," Giles exclaimed, "I like this interior, all of wood."

"All the native woods," Mary told him proudly, leading him from one room to the other, "white and yellow pine, sweet gum, maple, spruce, poplar, and oak."

"But there's one thing very much amiss," Margaret told Giles, "and it worries us both."

"And what is that?"

"Last summer's drought," explained Margaret. "Our tobacco. You know it was my plan to pay for the home with last summer's crop. And we have had no more than anyone else. Will it be all right, Giles, for our creditors to wait a whole year? "

"They'll just have to," Giles told her. "And don't worry," he comforted. "The creditors of all of us here will be waiting. Heaven forbid we have many droughts such as this summer's has been. Meanwhile, we'll all be paupers together. Cozy, eh?"

"Mercy on us," scolded Mary, "I don't see how you can be so frivolous about it, Giles. Still, we are not strangers to backbreaking debts."

Giles instantly knew her reference.

"Now Mary," he told her, "this is Maryland. No one will take your home from you. And if it will help any I can easily advance some—"

"Oh no, thank you kindly," Margaret stopped him. "Mary and I must manage on our own. We are not going to be a burden to you in any way. And as you so rightly say, Giles, in a twelvemonth all this will change."

Margaret could not know how truly she spoke, for long before the year was out quite a change came into their lives, from a most unexpected source and of a most unusual nature. And the change, indirectly, could be laid to the never-to-be-forgotten drought of the summer of 1639.

That drought, a hardship for many as to their money and food crops, was a great blessing to Father White.

From the very beginning of the colony Maryland had taken pains and no little expense to protect the Piscataway Indians from their native enemies, for of all the local tribes, they alone had been friendly to the settlement at St. Mary's.

Now the drought, too, was their enemy. Their corn crop was a total failure. So they asked the pale-faced Governor of the palefaces to send them enough corn to carry them over the winter and until the first spring harvest in 1640. Leonard Calvert responded immediately and generously.

Next thing he knew the Tayac, Chitomachon, Emperor of the Piscataways, asked him to send the Black Robe to their village of Kittamaquaandi to tell them about the Great Spirit. Of course the *Black* Robe was Father *White*.

The Governor's decision on this request was slower than the one about the corn.

Other Indians in Maryland and Virginia were causing a lot of trouble. The Maryland ones were stirred up, no doubt, by Claiborne. In Virginia, Opechancanough, brother and successor of Powhatan, had raided the colony and brutally killed 500 English. Governor William Berkeley sent a messenger to Maryland asking for an army of one hundred men. Berkeley had succeeded John Harvey as Governor of Virginia. Harvey had been recalled to England on the "evidence" of Claiborne's stories about him. You remember Harvey was friendly toward the Marylanders. This attitude did not suit Claiborne's evil schemes.

The Governor of Maryland almost laughed over the request of the Governor of Virginia.

He had recently commissioned Giles to raise an army of a hundred men on Kent to keep the Susquehannocks from attacking the Piscataways. The Susquehannocks were urged on by the Dutch in New Amsterdam and the Swedes in Delaware with arms and ammunition, because these two colonies wanted to see the Maryland colony fail and dissolve.

Leonard told Giles that if he couldn't get a hundred volunteers he must draft the men. Even by this device—it was called "impressment" then—Giles could muster only twenty unwilling, seemingly half-scared residents of Kent.

It was because of all these Indian disturbances that Leonard and the Council hesitated to let Father White go to the Piscataways. Not that this tribe was distrusted; but suppose they were attacked by their enemies? Finally, in the spring of 1640, they let Father White go.

Early in June he sent word to Leonard that he would like to see him as soon as possible at Patuxent in the village of Kittamaquaandi. This little Indian village lay between the Piscataway Creek and the rise of the Patuxent River on the western side of Chesapeake Bay, not more than thirty miles over land and water from Kent Island.

Leonard went at once. When he met Father White he noted that he looked exceptionally well and very happy. The wonderful news was that the Tayac, Chitomachon, had asked to be baptized.

"Beyond the slightest doubt," Father White told him, "Our Blessed Lord has smiled upon our mission."

"I am happy your labors have been so fruitful and so soon, and that you are safe and have not been harmed," Leonard told him.

"Harmed? By these innocent children of God? How can you!" Father White mildly remonstrated. "But I want you to know you have had a real part in this conversion!"

"In what manner?" asked Leonard.

"By sending supplies over this past winter. Last season's drought would have meant real suffering and famine had you not come to their aid."

"Tush!" said Leonard. "Neighbor helps neighbor in the wilderness."

"Not always, my son. And your generosity has made its

mark. Only a few days ago Chitomachon, calling his people to the council fire, told them no longer could he have faith in rocks, rivers, forests. What, he asked them, had these little gods done in their need? Then before them all he picked up a large stone and threw it into the heart of the fire, showing them his scorn for that which they have always considered a god. Then he spoke of the One God of the palefaces who had told the white man to help them in their need. He carried on at a great rate—all to this great result."

"I know you are satisfied it is not by food alone that they come to baptism, Father," said Leonard cautiously, "and if we have been a tool in your mission . . ."

"Now, my son, the Tayac wishes you, as equal to him in rank among the white men, to be his sponsor in baptism. He intends to make the ceremony an impressive occasion. He has begun work on an outdoor chapel for the event. He wishes you to bring your Council and all the prominent people in the Colony."

"We will make all his wishes come true," Leonard promised.

"He has one more wish," added Father White. "Since he is adopting the faith of the palefaces he wishes, for the occasion, also to adopt their dress."

Leonard's weather-tanned face broke into a broad smile.

"I am afraid, Father, that will be slightly ridiculous. Can you imagine the effect?"

Father White smiled, too. "I know," he said, "but we will never let them know how it seems to us. We will treat it all with the utmost sincerity, appreciating the compliment he intends to pay us."

"Naturally," Leonard agreed. "But fancy the great girth of Chitomachon encased in doublet and hose, waistcoat and

*"You must not refuse this tribute," said Father White.*

frills, a stiff white stock around that strong, muscular neck. You do not think you can dissuade him? "

"I would not if I could," Father White told him. "You must not refuse this tribute."

"Of course," Leonard said more soberly. Then as if only to himself, he added, "Where in all St. Mary's City can ever be found a pair of shoes to fit those tremendous, never-shod feet? "

"And it will be fitting to have Chitomachon's wife also clothed," Father White went on, ignoring Leonard's question.

"Fitting? Ah, yes," agreed Leonard, "if she can be fitted! "

"You find the thought amusing? Why don't you turn the project over to Mistress Margaret Brent? She will accomplish it if she has to create a gown by her own hand."

"Yes, Margaret," agreed Leonard. "She can meet any occasion with propriety and finesse. I will lay the whole matter in her hands."

The arranged date was the fifth of July. It turned out to be a very hot day.

A large delegation from St. Mary's journeyed by land and water to the Indian village to attend, getting very tired standing around in the sun or semi-shade, wiping their brows and wrists with their great linen handkerchiefs, the ladies fanning themselves very ineffectually, for the air, even in the shade, was unbearably warm. There was the Governor, Secretary Lewger and his wife, Captain Cornwayles, Thomas Greene, the James Neales—Mrs. Neale in one of her court dresses, a stiff, hot brocade—Cuthbert and Rose Fenwick, William Stone and his wife Virlinda, Sir Thomas and Lady Gerard, Margaret and Mary, and Giles from Kent. Only a few days previously Fulke had returned to England because their father, Sir Richard, was rapidly declining in health.

Before the arrival of the guests the Tayac had put on his ceremonial face paint. To the English he looked forbidding—more in the mood for war than the spiritual peace of baptism. But he wanted to pay them every compliment and look his very best, which to him meant swatches of white, yellow, and red paint on his cheeks, and a dark, indigo blue on his forehead. Leonard and Giles helped him into the European clothes he wished to wear.

As time went on the poor Indian looked more and more uncomfortable. The white stock around his neck began to crumble and wilt with perspiration, and streams of this ran down his face. He looked miserable, but stoically said nothing and smiled constantly. Only one thing he could not bear: the shoes and hose. Both were a tight fit, and with profuse apologies he removed them.

Meanwhile, Margaret and Mary had been struggling to get Mrs. Tayac into the dress they had brought for her. First they put on a shift and petticoats which Mrs. Tayac thought were enough. When they pulled the tight dress over her head she made quite a protest, but one word from Chitomachon silenced her. Margaret, taking pity on her, laced the bodice of the dress as loosely as possible. When they showed her the shoes they had brought for her, she made a great fuss and loudly called attention to her husband's unshod feet. This point she won: she remained barefooted.

So Chitomachon and his wife were ready for baptism. They stood before Father White, evidently hot and miserable in their European clothes, each holding a lighted candle. And after the baptism, Father White united them in Christian marriage. It was a solemn occasion.

During these events a little Indian girl, scarcely seven years old, and without a stitch of clothing, scampered about, in and out among the guests, pulling inquisitively at the ladies' dresses and staring at the gentlemen. Then, hiding behind one tree and then another, she would peek around, sometimes laughing, sometimes making funny faces. She was the eldest child of Chitomachon; and before the ceremonies were concluded Father White baptized her, too, naming her Mary.

Of all the English present, Giles had watched this child with amusement. You might think seeing her took him back to Larke Stoke and memories of their little sister Ann. But you would be wrong. The unkempt little girl with the exquisite teeth and the dirty face was, he realized, a princess, the Princess of the Piscataways. What a contrast to an English princess. And what an inheritance would someday be hers!

And what a surprise befell the three Brents before the day was over.

Father White and Leonard were first to learn of it. As Chitomachon was stripping off his hot European clothes as fast as he could, he told Father White and Leonard that he wanted the English to take his little daughter, now named Mary Kittamaquaandi, back to St. Mary's and make an Englishwoman out of her. He wanted her educated, disciplined—and this she certainly needed—and taught to be a lady. She would be seven in a few months, he said. Would they please make her a great lady, as great as she would be among her own people, teach her to read and write, to sew and cook the European way?

Father White immediately called Margaret and Mary to the rescue, so to say, and it sounds strange to say so, after the Tayac was all undressed and comfortable again! Giles hovered about the scene like a honeybee.

"You do well by her," he told Margaret when they were all in her shallop, returning to St. Mary's down Chesapeake Bay.

"And when she's twelve I'll marry her! "

"Oh, Giles!" complained Margaret, "it is too warm, the day has been too long and strenuous for your jests."

"Margaret is right," added Mary as she put a restraining hand on the little girl's arm; she was about to fall into the water as she leaned 'way over the edge. "You'd do better to help us face this—this pleasant, perhaps, but no small responsibility."

"What better can I do than to promise to marry her when you've made a lady of her? "

"Giles! In heaven's name, stop!" Margaret cried with irritation. "Be sensible. You know you've no such notion. Why, gracious alive, you're old enough to be her grandfather. You married to an Indian? Ridiculous!"

"Now just get that notion out of your pretty red head," Giles told Margaret gravely. "It is not ridiculous, and my age is not so great as to forbid it. In fact, I shall enter into an agreement with her father to marry her when she is twelve."

"You mustn't," cried Mary, near to tears.

"It just won't do. How do you know she'll love you, or that you will love her? "

"I love her now," Giles said, and reaching out his hand toward the little girl, he gently drew her to him and sat her on his knee. Her response was to rest her head on his shoulder, and with her hand in one of his she soon fell asleep.

Margaret looked at Giles disapprovingly. "You may make what arrangements you wish," she told him, "but I will legally adopt the child, and you cannot then marry her without my consent."

"I can't understand you, Giles," Mary chimed in. "You're always so circumspect, so conventional."

"I intend to remain so," Giles assured her curtly.

# 7.

# The Wealthiest Lady in Maryland

DOMESTIC details ran smoothly at the Freehold. The tobacco plantations produced abundantly after that first season of drought. Margaret opened a school at St. Mary's. The children liked it. An issue arose when she put Mary Kittamaquaandi in the first grade. The children were delighted; some parents were not. Margaret told them it was a Christian school. Mary remained.

But Margaret and Mary were not completely happy.

Things in the little world about them were awry; and in the big world across the ocean, England.

There a man named Cromwell was stirring up civil war against King Charles, one reason being that he was suspected of Catholic sympathies. Cromwell's followers were mostly Puritans and were called Roundheads because they cut their hair short. Cromwell called his army the Parliamentary Party.

Time and again Leonard's brother, Cecilius, the Lord Baltimore, planned to go to his colony of Maryland. But now with all this trouble he had to stay in England. In fact, he was placed under bond not to leave the realm. Of course he remained loyal to the King. He never saw Maryland. And, deprived of his presence and advice, Leonard's cares grew ever heavier.

All this trouble in England was one source of worry and discontent for the Brent sisters; then there was the trouble about Giles.

One fine day late in 1642 Giles found himself on trial for

sedition. Who stirred up this trouble? Although John Lewger, as "Attorney for the Lord Baltimore," made the charges, Giles never doubted for a moment but that Claiborne was at the bottom of it. Now that the trouble in England was growing, Claiborne was becoming bolder in his feud against the Catholics of Maryland.

Just before this storm broke over his head Giles deeded to Margaret everything he owned in Maryland. This took place October 10, 1642, the very same day the Governor was being ". . . informed of some passages and demeanors of Mr. Giles Brent upon the Isle of Kent, which gave . . . cause to suspect some intents and desires of his to disaffect that Island, and withdraw it into sedition."

Leonard had absolute trust in his friend and refused to give the matter his attention. But Lewger "informed" the court in such detail against Giles that Leonard had to let it stand in the record.

The deed of all Giles's properties, "real and personal," made Margaret the wealthiest lady in Maryland. It was witnessed by Captain Thomas Cornwayles, William Luddington and William Naufone. When it was signed and witnessed, all Giles had left were the clothes on his back.

Margaret was inclined to be depressed by her added responsibilities. When Fulke had had to return to England, he had given her his power of attorney over his Maryland properties and entrusted their whole management to her judgments and decisions. Now Giles's holdings, far more extensive than Fulke's, were hers too.

And she had other worries.

A great deal of tobacco was owed to her and she had not been able to collect these debts through the lawyers she had engaged to represent her in court. First it was Edward Parker who had failed her, then Thomas Greene. Her experiences with both these gentlemen were discouraging. She discussed her concern with Leonard.

"I think there is nothing for it but that I be my own lawyer," she told him anxiously, watching his face for his immediate reaction. "Granted I am not learned in the law, at least I should be able to do better than those two who are, and have so failed me. Do you think my appearance before the bar will be unbecoming?"

If he did think so, Leonard was not of a mind to tell her just that. Instead, he said, "It should be a challenge to our gentlemen to be more persevering in their pursuit of the law. And you are far and above many a man's mind among us in your qualities of intellect and ability with argument. But . .

"But? Go on, Leonard."

"I am sure you surmise such an action on your part will set many tongues to wagging."

"Ah, bother," said Margaret. "Tongues in idle heads."

"Agreed," said Leonard.

"But I have no wish to make a spectacle of myself. That is my concern. Will it be very dreadful, Leonard? Now with all my added responsibilities, there will be a great deal of court business. Unless I appear for myself, for Giles, perhaps, and certainly for Fulke, it is all going to be very expensive, exceptionally so if I pay lawyers' fees to lose every case I bring up. I well know, if I begin this practice of appearing myself, it will be a reflection upon Edward Parker, Thomas Greene and others whom I might employ. Yet, already, in private hearings before the court I have won judgments in my favor in the two cases I originally gave these lawyers to handle for me."

"Everything you say is in favor of what you propose,"

Leonard told her. "In my opinion you should proceed as you have outlined. And as for the possible wagging tongues, bear in mind Giles is a conspicuous member of the Council, in my full confidence and Cecilius's, too. Further, many realize how highly I esteem both Mary and yourself. I doubt tongues will dare to wag too vigorously for your peace of mind."

"Thank you, Leonard," she replied, blushing slightly and dropping her eyelids. "I know if censure does not start at the top it cannot live long. And I will feel so much better to be able to handle court matters for myself."

But as events unfolded Margaret's scorn of gossips was to be put to an immediate test. And while she lost no time in taking to court matters involving debts due her or Fulke or Giles's properties now hers, it was not on this score that the gossip arose.

In fact, very little attention was paid to Margaret's affairs in the light of John Lewger's charges against Giles. He demanded that Giles be brought to public trial for sedition.

This whole affair which lasted for months was a source of acute humiliation to all three Brents. Even little Mary Kittamaquaandi, unable to understand the full gravity of the matter, but realizing "enemies" were out to hurt Giles, knew a deep indignation toward "those bad palefaces," as she called the court and jury.

Lewger's charges covered pages and pages in the provincial records. All boiled down to one sentence; they charged that Leonard had told Giles to raise an army to ward off the Susquehannocks, that he had only made a half try to do so and failed, and that as a result the colony was in disgrace and had been put to a lot of "fruitless expense."

Margaret flared when she heard the long-winded accusation read in open court. That evening she told Giles,

*The whole mess dragged on for more than two months*

"You should go straight to the King and see to it that Lewger retracts every word openly, and then is jailed for slandering your good name and character."

"Margaret's right, Giles," said Mary. "I'll back her up in that."

But Giles was cool and confident although his heart was warmed by his sisters' loyalty.

"You just leave this all to me," he said gratefully. "I've always suspected Lewger for a gossipy, meddlesome old woman. I will win this conflict and he will suffer for it without my ever raising a hand or saying one word in his disfavor."

"You must not keep still," said Margaret.

"I shan't have to," Giles promised her. "And I believe time will reveal the tongue of William Claiborne behind all this flurry with Lewger taking his information from him."

"Can you prove that? " Margaret wanted to know.

"Probably not," Giles replied. "But I can believe it in my heart."

"I will find him in the light of the full moon, chirped in Mary Kittamaquaandi, "and from behind a great tree where he will not see me I will send a poison arrow in his heart. For my protector I will do this."

Giles put his arm about the child, kissed her forehead, and then said gently, "And then he will die, my little one, and never live to regret his unkindness. Would it not be better for him to live years and years to wish he had never slandered me? "

"Would that be better, truly?" she asked, puzzled.

"It would please the Great Spirit better," Giles told her quietly, "if you will let Him Who knows all and sees all punish the one who would disgrace me. Better let it be that way," he concluded.

When the child was out of earshot he asked his sisters, "There's not the remotest chance that child has any poisoned arrows hidden about the house, is there? "

The trouble dragged through the courts late into the fall. Lewger brought his charges three times and three times Giles answered them. Lewger wished the charges to remain on the permanent records but that only memoranda be kept of Giles's replies. As Attorney for the Lord Baltimore, Lewger very nearly won this point, but Giles was finally able to get his responses into the records, too. And on November 8 he told the court that if, as he expected, it would be proved that he had been slandered, he would go straight to His Majesty for redress.

The foreman of the jury called to try Giles was James Neale. Perhaps this threat of Giles carried weight with the twelve men charged to "truly try and true verdict give" in the case. The jury found Giles "Not Guilty." This verdict was given November 28, 1642.

John Lewger was furious over his defeat. On Monday, December 2, he opened the matter all over again, repeating once more his charges and once again ordering Giles to appear and answer. This was too much for Giles's patience, which all through the fall had been exemplary. He appeared on December 12 and for the fourth time repeated his answer to the charges.

The court realized that Lewger must be stopped once and for all, so as a body, Lewger only dissenting, the members of the court voted to dismiss the case against Giles "without day," which meant it could never again be brought up in that court.

Four days later, on December 16, Leonard showed his confidence in Giles by sending him back to Kent as military commander of the Island.

By the deed Giles gave Margaret she became responsible for all the debts he had incurred before October 10, 1642. Among these was a large sum due three persons in Virginia.

"What is this tremendous total for?" she asked Giles.

"Tremendous? Poof! How you do talk for a rich lady!" Giles raised his bushy eyebrows and turned his head to one side, watching her hesitantly. "Why not just pay without question? " he suggested.

"That is asking a lot," Margaret told him frankly. "Come, Giles, surely I have a right to know what I am paying for? "

"Well, for the sake of your peace of mind—"

"Bother that," Margaret told him quickly. "I don't believe that is to be found anywhere. How can one have peace of mind with a civil war threatening in England?"

"Exactly! That is the very point." Giles studied her carefully. "I do believe you've felt it, too."

"What?"

"Oh, come, you and I do not mince words between us. You know we may one day wish to move from Maryland."

Margaret's shoulders drooped and she sank lower into the chair by the window where she was sitting. She looked at Giles sadly.

"I have refused to let myself form that thought even in silent words."

"But in our troubled times anything may happen. So, against the possible day I have purchased land in Virginia, and I intend to buy a great deal more. Virginia will be our refuge. Now this which I have already purchased is for you. It is yours. I have an option on the adjoining tract north of your property."

"So that is what this sum is for? But Giles —" Margaret

paused. "Think you we will be welcome in Virginia? You were not in 1625."

"That was years ago. Things are changing. I know we will be welcome. I am on the most friendly terms with Sir William Berkeley, the present Governor. I have his personal assurances we will not be molested for the matter of our faith. We will have peace in Virginia, Margaret. I promise you."

"Peace!"

"For a fact, why not call your home, your new home in Virginia, just that? What better name for it than 'Peace'? "

Margaret looked at Giles dubiously.

" 'Twould be a wonderful name if it could be true. Meanwhile, I will pay the debt for the land, and promptly."

"Good," said Giles. "And as soon as an opportunity presents we will visit Mr. Stafford on Aquia Creek there, and I will negotiate for my tract next to yours. That's where I'll spend my retirement."

"Retirement? I can barely think of you retiring, Giles— you who are always so foremost in provincial matters."

"Ah, but a man looks forward to his retirement."

A familiar whistle outside the window diverted their attention.

"That will be Leonard," said Margaret, as Giles went to open the door. As he did so Leonard was tying his horse to the hitching post close by the broad stone stoop.

"Come in and welcome," Giles said. "Margaret and I are here alone."

"Good," said Leonard. "I want to talk to you both."

He took a chair near the hearth which was aglow with the embers of a dying fire.

"This is a bit awkward," he told Giles. "I expected to find you at your own house and hoped to find Margaret—er—alone."

"I understand," Giles told him. "State your business with me if Margaret may hear it, too, and then I shall leave you two."

"Indeed she may," Leonard replied. "She will otherwise hear it directly from you. It is this: I am forced to the decision to go at once to see Cecilius."

"Home?" Margaret asked, leaving the word in mid-air, so to say, for it shocked her to find she still thought of England as home.

"I must have personal consultations with Cecilius," Leonard resumed, taking no notice of the word. "Letters take too long and there's never an assurance they will reach their destination."

"Better perhaps as matters are now not to put too much in writing in any event," Giles suggested.

"Quite right," agreed Leonard. "And now my business with you, Giles, is to tell you I want to leave you acting Governor in my absence. Will you so serve? "

"Leonard!" Margaret exclaimed, a happy smile on her face. "Do you realize what you do? What will Mr. Lewger think?"

"My concern is what Giles thinks," Leonard told her, returning her smile. Well he knew that such an appointment would be a final vindication of Giles.

Giles was evidently moved. The muscles in his cheeks twitched and he rubbed his chin vigorously. He put out his right hand toward Leonard, who grasped it firmly.

"You do me great honor," he told Leonard gravely, "and I promise I will not disappoint you."

"I would not expect you to," Leonard answered.

Giles spoke to Margaret without turning away from Leonard. "How about a cup of your fine Madeira to toast the Lord Baltimore and his brother?"

There was no answer. Both men turned about. But

Margaret was not in the room. She had slipped out the door into the refreshing coolness of the early April evening. She was so touched that Leonard had appointed Giles she could barely keep from weeping. She just had to be alone.

But she was not long alone. A whinny from Leonard's horse warned her that he was close behind her. She turned around to face him.

"Oh, Leonard, that you should place such confidence in Giles after the horrible Lewger charges."

"I have always trusted him," Leonard told her.

She sat down on the stone stoop, inviting Leonard with a gesture of her hand to sit beside her.

"You know," he said presently in a quiet voice, "I shall be gone at least a year, perhaps two, who can tell? "

"Yes, Leonard."

"That means nothing to you, Margaret? "

"It means you will be sorely missed."

"I am not asking for bouquets and applause," he told her, "I am only asking you, Mistress Margaret Brent, if this absence will not—does not give you pause—to—imagine, Margaret, months and months and months without—"

"Oh, Leonard, please, please," Margaret begged.

Leonard sighed audibly.

"I see," he said dejectedly. "I had hoped—"

"But I told you when first we came, Leonard, not to hope."

"You were homesick then—a thousand things on your mind. This is the last time, Margaret. I am desperate. Will you, will you marry me and return with me to England to be near me while I am away from Maryland? Margaret? "

"You force it from me—the hurt I would spare you, have tried always to spare you. No, Leonard, no, no, no! Oh, why have you made me say this?"

Margaret's voice broke. Quickly she left him, ran into the house, up the broad staircase, and into her own room.

A few days later, on the eleventh of April, 1643, John Lewger administered the oath of office to Giles. He was very grim and disapproving about it. He told Giles to put his left hand on the Gospels, to raise his right hand, and "repeat after me." Giles promised to defend the rights and interests of the Lord Baltimore "according to his heart and conscience."

On the fifteenth Leonard sailed for England which he reached three months later, in mid-July.

# 8.

# Another Scoundrel

COLONIAL affairs had run smoothly since Leonard's departure until, a few weeks before Christmas, a ship called the *Reformation* arrived at St. Mary's City. The master was Richard Ingle. He said he had come "to trade." It soon developed he had come to trade in trouble rather than in merchandise.

Richard Ingle was a Roundhead sympathizer—some believed him an undercover agent for the Parliamentary Party. He held a commission from the Brents' old neighbor the Earl of Warwick, Lord Robert Rich, now a follower of Cromwell.

The *Reformation* also brought mail from England—Christmas mail and packages. Among the letters was one addressed to Giles, but intended for his sisters as well. It was from Sir Richard. The Brents were shocked to note the frailty of their father's handwriting which had always been bold and strong with lots of flourishes. This hand was weak, a light scrawl, the lines all going downhill.

The message was brief: and another shock, though not unpleasant.

"As of the final day of this month of July in the year of Our Lord sixteen hundred and forty-three," he wrote, "with my paternal blessing your sister Ann and Leonard Calvert have been united in holy wedlock."

"Ann!" Margaret exclaimed, stunned.

"Well, at last he's got one of my sisters," said Giles. "And I am well pleased."

"Ann! It's not possible she's old enough," Mary mused thoughtfully.

"She's sixteen," said Margaret, "and Leonard old enough to be her father. How could he?"

"Now look here," Giles scolded. "Ann has taken after you since she could toddle—has your same red hair and blue eyes, the same fair complexion.

"Give Leonard credit for loving her," put in Mary timidly.

"You are making me miserable," Margaret told Giles. "I want them to be happy, both of them. Let us rejoice our sister will be here with us and that our tie with the Calverts is this much stronger."

"All I can say is I pray the Good Lord that Leonard will not take too much time to dillydally with romancing. How this Ingle creature ever fell into our path I could not guess. But he spells trouble. Reports come to me daily of treasonable remarks he makes about His Majesty's government and person. I don't like it. He gives out he is here to trade. Zounds! To trade in treason!"

"He's barely landed," Margaret told him. "How can you be so alarmed?"

"He's been here long enough to stir up unrest and uncertainty. He prates the monarchy in England is doomed, that even now Parliament may be the ruling power. He promises the 'tyrannical rule of the Lord Baltimore' will come to an end any day a ship arrives with news of Parliament's victory. He's got the people uneasy. Even the members of the Council are murmuring in their sleeves."

"Why don't you stop him? " asked Mary.

"How can I without grounds?" Giles told her crossly. "Much comes to my ears, but when I ask the informers to write down what they have heard and swear an oath to its truth they run and hide as from the devil. Only one sworn statement have I got, from old Elijah Harris."

"The one whose house burned to the ground?" asked Mary, a trace of terror in her voice.

"Exactly. And that was after his statement to me. You can figure that out, can't you?"

"I see why you wish for Leonard's return," Margaret agreed.

"Precious little chance of it," rejoined Giles, "with romancing on his mind."

A few weeks after this talk with his sisters, Giles was forced to act. He had promised to protect the interests and rights of the Lord Baltimore, and to allow Richard Ingle to continue at large with his disturbing tongue was not a fulfillment of this promise.

So, on January 18, 1643, signed a warrant for Ingle's arrest. Edward Parker, the sheriff, was out of the city at the time and Giles deputized William Hardige to act in his stead. He also commissioned Captain Cornwayles and James Neale to assist Hardige. The most difficult detail was the fact that as yet no jail had been built at St. Mary's. The only jail was "the sheriff's two hands."

"That Ingle will slip through Parker's weak fingers like milk through muslin," Margaret told Giles. "And I don't understand why you should have put the Captain into it, Giles. What is the matter with you? You must know the Captain has been harboring Ingle at Cross Manor as a distinguished guest. You have made a big, big mistake."

"You are making one right now," Giles told her indignantly. "It is I who am the acting Governor, not you, Margaret, and I will thank you to respect my judgment. I have put the Captain in his present position to give him pause to think.

You are right, he has shown too much favor to the traitor, and it has caused concern and confusion. What I have done I have done to correct the bad impression he has given—all unconsciously, I sincerely believe."

A week or ten days passed with no action on the warrant. Ingle remained at Cross Manor as did his host Captain Cornwayles. Then Parker returned to the City and Giles insisted he proceed with the arrest. This was accomplished by a ruse which led Ingle to Smith's Tavern in the company of the Captain and James Neale. There Parker served the warrant and took Ingle to his own house where he locked him up in Mrs. Parker's cold cellar.

Giles was pleased and gratified, and instructed John Lewger to draw proper charges against Ingle so he might be tried. Meanwhile, he had the *Reformation* seized and held by the local militia.

The evening following these events, Giles went to the Freehold to have a talk with Margaret. She was not in a mood for his mission when Giles told her, "It's about my little Princess. I want to marry her at once."

"Not tonight, Giles," Margaret told him. "I am too weary to parry with you. I've just come from Kent Fort Manor, and have been over the spring-planting plans with Tidd. I can't do justice to this matter."

"You have only to give your consent," Giles told her.

"But she is barely ten years old. You promised her father you'd not marry her until she is twelve. What would people think—you the acting Governor, marrying a native child only ten. Giles, what is the matter with you?"

"The matter is with her people. It is now three years since Chitomachon's death. Mary Kittamaquaandi is not receiving her inheritance. I must secure it for her. Unless she is legally my wife, I have no cause to proceed to this end."

"You know, Giles, I've always had a great love and profound respect for you," Margaret told her brother soberly, "but now I don't know what's come over you—or has something come over me? How can you come here in pursuit of your own interests—really greedy interests, I am bound to say—when you have been so remiss about the Ingle matter. I, for one, believe our whole Colony to be in the most dire danger right this minute."

"Zounds!" exclaimed Giles. "I have always had great love and respect for you, too, as my most clear-thinking, even brilliant sister, uncannily so for a woman. But you have roused my ire now; you have been listening to old wives' gossip. With Captain Cornwayles in full command of the situation—"

"Is he?" Margaret demanded. "Do you know this for fact, or only hearsay? Everyone knows he has become Ingle's ardent friend. Everyone but you. Gossip, indeed! Oh, Giles, in the name of heaven get about the city and make sure all is well."

"I demand you put these foolish fears out of your mind and listen to what I have to say about Mary Kittamaquaandi," Giles told her, his temper rising rapidly. "I should never have let myself get in this predicament—having to ask your consent. All I want to do is marry her so I can fight for her inheritance."

"Which, in land, amounts to almost the entire area of Cecilius's patent," Margaret told him bluntly.

"I have no least intention of taking her for wife," Giles continued as though Margaret had not interrupted, "until she is sixteen. But I must marry her at once as a matter of material expediency."

A loud, imperative knock on the heavy oak door

*Margaret saw the face of Edward Parker*

interrupted their quarrel.

"Egad!" complained Giles. "Stay where you are," he told Margaret. "I'll get this."

And he crossed to the door, opening the upper half.

By the light of hearth and candles Margaret saw the face of Edward Parker. She caught her breath, bit her lower lip.

"Well, Parker," Giles demanded abruptly. "Right rotten news, sir." Parker was so agitated he was almost stammering. "Ingle has escaped."

"Why the devil come and tell me? Why aren't you after him?"

"T-t-that I c-c-can't, sir," Parker blurted. "T-t-the *Reformation* is headed out to sea. It's a good w-w-w-wind . . ."

"By the saints, it's not possible!" Giles roared. "You blithering milksop. Get the Captain to me at once. Tell him . . ."

Parker shook his head violently.

"The devil with you," Giles cried. "I order you to get the Captain."

Parker's temper flared then. "The Captain is aboard the *Reformation* himself. A passenger. He has deserted the Province."

"You will be whipped for such a lie against . . ."

"He travels as Ingle's guest by his own free choice and, on my soul, this is no doing of mine. I released Ingle in the company of the Captain, and it is by your orders, sir, that the Captain's commission outranked my office. From the beginning you did not trust me—'twas you commissioned the Captain and Neale to assist me."

"Do you have witnesses for what you say? " demanded Giles.

"One," returned Parker. "James Neale."

# 9.

# Trouble, Trouble

THE shocking event of Ingle's escape and the Captain's departure from the Province did not deter Giles from his intention of marrying Mary Kittamaquaandi as soon as possible.

He had been frank with Margaret. His motivation was material. But this is not to say he did not love the little Indian Princess. He did. Everyone did. To Margaret and Mary she had become as close as one of their own sisters. With grace and intelligence she had adapted herself to English ways. She seemed much older than her years because she was so wise in natural things—growing things, trees, plants, animals. Her spirits were always gay and happy. And she was loyally devoted to her English guardians, including Giles.

"I just don't feel your plan will work," Margaret told Giles the May morning when he brought his question to the fore again. "I believe that when Chitomachon gave Mary to us he forfeited her right to any inheritance from the Piscataways. But . . ."

"Then let me marry her," Giles urged, "let me prove you right or wrong. As it is now I can do nothing to secure what is rightfully hers; as her husband I have a chance. And the child will not leave your roof; she will be with you another six years, I promise."

So it was arranged with Margaret's full consent. Giles and the Princess of the Piscataways were married quietly on the lawn of the Freehold one mild morning in May when the spring blossoms sent a heavy, sweet fragrance on the soft breezes that blew off the sunlit surface of the river.

Giles did his best after that to secure for his Princess that which her father, Chitomachon, had willed she should have. But her people disowned her, rebuffed Giles, and proved Margaret right. Even the Lord Baltimore frowned on his efforts. In the end they all came to naught.

Shortly after the quiet event of the wedding, all being calm in the Province, Giles decided on a brief visit to Virginia. Sir William Berkeley would leave for England the end of June and Giles would like to give him, for the Lord Baltimore, copies of the records covering the Ingle affair.

He suggested that Margaret go with him.

"Wouldn't you like to see your property on Aquia Creek?" he asked her. "A good opportunity to meet your future neighbors."

"You seem so sure we shall move to Virginia."

"Aye, that I am," Giles told her soberly. "I wager before 1650 we will have left Maryland. It will not long be what we hoped from our very first dreams. All good things come to an end—this you know."

Margaret did not like to hear Giles say such things, but she very much liked the Virginia tract he had purchased for her. It was peaceful and the neighboring people were kind and friendly without being familiar. They seemed anxious for the Brents to settle among them. Margaret spent hours of contentment in Virginia that lovely month of June. In fact, Giles was loathe to take her back to Maryland and its inevitable problems. But toward the latter part of August he felt he could not stay away any longer considering his responsibilities as acting governor.

Early in the morning of August 26 they reached St. Mary's

City. And before that day was over the long-smoldering feud between Giles and John Lewger flared up. The result was that Giles fired Lewger from his post of Secretary and Attorney for his Lordship.

The whole business was over the same old Susquehannocks trouble. Lewger was bound and determined to have an army snuff out this troublesome tribe, and the moment Giles had gone to Virginia he forged Giles's name to a commission to Henry Fleete to raise up an army and exterminate the Susquehannocks. That was on June 18, 1644.

But the humiliation of Mr. Lewger was of short duration, for in September Leonard returned to the Province—without his wife—and brought with him new commissions for all members of the Council including the Secretary, John Lewger. However, Lewger was not reappointed his Lordship's Attorney. That commission was in Leonard's name and held by him from then on. This fact gave him two votes in the Assembly, one for himself and one for the Lord Baltimore.

As soon as possible after his return he spent an evening with the Brents.

"I'm heartsick you could not bring Ann with you," Margaret told Leonard as they settled in the garden under the maple trees which were just beginning to turn to their fall fashion in colors.

"Yes, we've been looking forward to reunion, to having Ann here where we could be close to each other," added Mary.

"Not one of you is as heartsick as I am," Leonard told them, "but the doctor assured me it would be taking her life in my hands to subject her to the hazards of the voyage before our second child is born. In another twelve-month, God willing, I will return to Larke Stoke for her and both babies. It was not easy to leave Ann and my son."

Not one of them could know that warm September evening that God would not be willing. In another twelvemonth many changes would come about.

At the time, however, all was comparatively quiet in the Colony. Richard Ingle was an unpleasant memory, Captain Cornwayles was missed but rarely mentioned. Claiborne, as was his habit, was making trouble on Kent—so much that Mary, to whom Margaret had given Kent Fort Manor for her very own, felt insecure there and was again living at the Freehold. Leonard had posted on the Mulberry Tree a notice to the effect that Claiborne was an open enemy of the Province and no one was to have anything to do with him.

The Assembly was due to meet at St. Mary's City in February, 1645. It was in session on St. Valentine's Day when Edward Parker broke in upon the proceedings with an urgent message for the Governor.

"There are ships rounding the point at St. Inigoes," he whispered in Leonard's ear. "How many it cannot be seen because of the mist. But this we know by our glasses: the ships come armed. In the lead is the *Reformation!*"

Leonard did not keep the information secret.

He told the Assembly at once, and with the speed of lightning gave orders to those present to leave for their homes and families, to gather their arms and ammunition. They were to report to Captain Giles Brent at the Fort as soon as might be, bringing their families there for safety's sake. He warned that in all probability there would be bloodshed.

Aside to Giles he said, behind his hand, "I will go to the Freehold. Trust your dear ones to me. I will get them to the Fort at once."

"A better move for you," Giles told him sharply, "will be to escape immediately to Virginia. Ingle, no doubt, comes with much presumed authority and will be after you first to imprison you. If you wish to preserve Maryland in the future, you must leave now, this instant. You have just said you have put me in full command. This is my order to you. I will take care of my sisters and little Mary."

Leonard protested this direction but Giles was adamant. "You do not know Ingle. I do. Take my shallop. It is tied to my wharf not a stone's throw from here. Go, in the name of heaven—now!"

Within the hour Giles found time to give his sisters similar orders in person. Margaret, too, protested. Why, she demanded, should she run like a coward? But Giles hushed her with a severity he had never used before with her, which so dumfounded her that she obeyed him instantly. So it was that before nightfall, Leonard Calvert, Governor of Maryland, was beyond the reach of Richard Ingle and Giles's family were safe, too, in Virginia.

Giles had acted wisely in thus banishing Leonard from the Province. For Ingle came ashore just before sundown with a well-armed, rowdy army, claiming Maryland in the name of Parliament. His men routed the city, set fire to many homes and invaded St. Gabriel's in search of Leonard. Not finding him, they confiscated all the colonial records and the great seal of the Province. The records were thrown to the flames, the seal into the bay. Ingle then marched on the Fort.

Before dawn Giles, John Lewger, Father White and Father Copley, another Jesuit priest who had come to Maryland on the same ship with the Brents in 1638, were prisoners of Ingle. And before another sundown these four, with many others, were on board the *Reformation*, headed out to sea and England. The priests were put in chains and secured on the open deck of the ship. This was a terrible hardship for Father

*Giles so dumbfounded her, she obeyed instantly*

White who was then almost sixty. The civilians were kept in their cabins under armed guard.

In Maryland all who would not take an oath against the Lord Baltimore were robbed of their possessions, their homes burned to the ground and they themselves left to wander about the countryside like lost souls. Those who submitted peaceably to the invaders, acknowledging the sovereignty of Parliament, were unmolested. And after several weeks of pillage and looting, of boisterous, drunken raids and wanton destruction, Ingle and his men retired to St. Inigoes, a point of land five miles south of the city. Here they built a fort and remained to themselves, sending their prisoners now and then into the city for supplies—corn, cattle and dairy products.

Leonard, during this time, had established himself at Kequotan, in Virginia, on the northeast shore of the James River. Many Marylanders joined him here. And it was here, less than a week after the sudden invasion, that the Brent sisters learned of Giles's arrest and deportation to England.

Matters remained in this uncertain state for eighteen months.

At the time of Leonard's escape, Richard Kemp was acting Governor of Virginia during the absence of Sir William Berkeley in England. Almost overnight the general attitude of hostility which the Virginia colony had held for Maryland changed into one of sincere sympathy, but Richard Kemp hesitated to give Leonard official assistance. He feared a hangman's noose about his neck if, by helping the Governor of Maryland, he should offend the present government in England. He would wait and let Governor Berkeley assume the full responsibility.

Berkeley returned to his Colony in the fall of 1646, and

with him were Giles and John Lewger. When they arrived in England they had escaped their captors and made their way to the Lord Baltimore, who had protected them until they could return to Maryland. Governor Berkeley was determined that Virginia would help Maryland and lost no time issuing a call for volunteers. He promised Leonard a formidable army.

If Leonard could have paid an army in English money, in no time at all he could probably have mustered more than a hundred men. But he had no English money. Nor could he be sure Cecilius would be able to send him any, for his brother had lost much, by confiscation, in the Civil War. This included Baltimore in County Longford, Ireland, which had been taken by the Roundheads at the very beginning of Cromwell's activities. But to each volunteer Leonard promised his "hire & wages" would be paid out of the Maryland livestock or personal property of the Lord Baltimore. If, when they landed at St. Mary's, resistance was met, the soldiers could take anything they could lay their hands on, every man for himself. But if there was no resistance, they would be paid with cattle or land.

On these terms Leonard finally gathered a considerable number of men willing to follow him. He armed and provisioned them at his own expense. To do this took just about all that he owned.

Meantime, Maryland had a so-called Governor. His name was Edward Hill. He was not a member of the Colony, but a Virginian whom some of the people in St. Mary's City had persuaded to assume the governorship. To make it seem legal and proper, the commission by which he held the office was forged with the name of Leonard Calvert, and dated July 30, 1646, "in Virginia." Of course Leonard was kept informed of all these activities by his faithful spies. It was from such sources he learned that Edward Hill had called the Assembly to meet in St. Mary's City in December, 1646.

All his preparations made, he waited for a dark night to approach the city by water. The following morning, well before daylight, Leonard and his army of volunteers from Virginia landed on Maryland soil. All remained under cover until the hour when the Assembly would be in session. Then at the head of his men Leonard boldly marched through the city to St. Gabriel's where the Assembly sat. They entered without resistance, and took prisoner Hill and everyone present.

Never did a surprise invasion meet with such a reception. The entire Assembly, every man his prisoner, rose to give Leonard Calvert, the rightful Governor, a standing ovation. They cheered and applauded for several minutes.

Here and there, in isolated sections of the city, Leonard's army had a few skirmishes with Ingle's men. But Ingle, getting wind of Leonard's return, escaped to the *Reformation*, which immediately put out to sea.

His whole escapade had been a tremendous hoax, for not yet was Parliament the sovereign rule in England! Although he had suffered defeat in battle with Cromwell's men, Charles I was still on the throne and the Lord Baltimore still rightfully the proprietor of his Colony in the New World.

Generously Leonard pardoned all who had taken part in the rebellion. He sent Edward Hill back to Virginia, continued the Assembly in session j and quickly restored law and order in the colony.

# 10.

# His Lordship's Attorney

A S MIGHT be expected, while Leonard had been an exile in Virginia and Maryland was under the unlawful oppression of Richard Ingle, William Claiborne had quickly occupied the Island of Kent. He ruled it with an iron hand, pretending he was the lord and owner of the whole domain. He was completely in control there in December, 1646, when Leonard recovered St. Mary's. And as the weeks went by he gave no indication that he would retire. So there was nothing for Leonard to do but gather his army, lay his plans, and set out to recapture Kent for Cecilius. So grave by this time had become the troubles in England, with King Charles now a prisoner in the hands of Parliament, he could expect no help or advice from his brother.

He timed his operation for April, 1647. Once again his army met with no resistance.

What is more, the moment Claiborne heard of its approach, true to his cowardly nature he fled to the safety of Virginia. The inhabitants of Kent gave Leonard as great a welcoming ovation as had the Assembly at St. Mary's. Without the least hesitation everyone took the oath of allegiance to Lord Baltimore. And on April 16, as he had done in the city, Leonard pardoned all on Kent who had committed "crimes of rebellion."

When Leonard returned to St. Mary's early in May, Margaret told him he ought to take a good rest.

"You don't look well at all," she said, concerned. "Perhaps this is the time for you to go back to Larke Stoke and get Ann and the children. The long voyage would give you a good chance to recover from all the hardships and worries you've been through."

"I could hardly go now," Leonard told her, "with the army to pay off. I must settle all their accounts first. Some want to stay with us, and they shall have land. Others must be paid in tobacco or cattle, however they may wish. And for a truth I am worried about the payments."

"Worried? "

"Well, yes, I've exhausted everything I have. I must pay them from Cecilius's holdings. But during the occupation his lands have been neglected, his cattle stolen and probably killed. I am going to search diligently for any heads that may carry his brand, but I am sure Ingle has done away with all his stock. And as for his tobacco! My brother, the Lord Baltimore, believe it or not as you will, is a poor man in his own province."

"We have all suffered," Margaret told him. "Don't worry yourself so. You look haggard and worn. Ann would be fretful could she see you."

"I wonder," put in Giles, who generally could be found at the Freehold now since Ingle had burned his fine White House, "if you should let the army go just yet? You are aware of the rumors that Edward Hill is planning to come back and resume the governorship?"

"I had hoped you would not mention that before your sisters," Leonard told him. "They have had enough alarms. And for that matter I put no credence in those rumors, but the army will have to stay until I can pay every man—and, naturally, the longer I have to hold it the more I will have to pay!"

Giles looked at Margaret as though asking her a question.

Finding the expression in her eyes wholly sympathetic, he said to Leonard, "If need be we, Margaret and myself, will be glad to help you with that burden. You may repay us as time and favorable crops of tobacco permit. Let us help you over this worry."

"It is Cecilius you would be helping."

"And we would have no objection to helping such a loyal friend," Margaret reassured him.

But as events worked themselves out, Leonard never paid his army at all. That was left for others to do. For early in June he fell seriously ill. Today his trouble would be called ptomaine poisoning, but then such a disease was not known.

Margaret and Mary went to St. Gabriel's to nurse him and were with him constantly. They watched him grow worse and worse. Margaret, in desperation, sent to Virginia for Dr. Waldron. But he could not help Leonard.

On the morning of the ninth of June he himself realized that he would not recover. He sent for Thomas Greene, and in the presence of Margaret and Mary and Giles, appointed Greene to serve as Governor only until Cecilius should make his own appointment. And then, turning to Margaret, in the presence of the others, he said, "Take all and pay all."

These five small words were the most fateful ever spoken to Margaret. They meant she would be the executrix of Leonard Calvert's estate, that she would inherit everything he owned and all his debts. These included those he assumed for Cecilius and which he would have satisfied from the Lord Baltimore's properties, for in Maryland he was his Lordship's Attorney. After his death, this title and its responsibilities would fall to Margaret, too.

Just six hours after Leonard told Margaret, "Take all and pay all," he died. Margaret and Mary were with him and also

Thomas Greene.

Margaret could not believe the end had come. She sat by Leonard's bedside a long, long time. Finally Mary said, "You'd better come, dear. It's all over. We can do nothing more here now."

Margaret looked at her pleadingly, her eyes swimming with tears which streamed down her cheeks. Slowly she got up, accepting Mr. Greene's helping hand. She walked between Mary and him to the door of Leonard's room. And there she turned to look once more at the still form on the bed.

Swallowing hard, she turned to Mary and sadly shook her head.

"This is Maryland's greatest blow," she said in a choking voice. "It will never, never be the same again."

Then she covered her face with her hands and, crying bitterly, left the room.

Ten days later, on June 19, Thomas Greene reported to the provincial court all that transpired at Leonard's bedside the morning of the day of his death, assuring the court that he was "in perfect memory" at the time of his final instructions. On this same day Margaret asked the court for formal letters of administration so she could proceed to settle Leonard's affairs and somehow pay the army he had brought from Virginia and which would no longer be needed.

As soon as it was known she was the executrix of Governor Calvert's estate, she was besieged by persons who claimed Leonard owed them various sums of tobacco. In going over his accounts she found that even more was owed *to* him. She had to appear in court over and over again to try to collect.

And very soon after she assumed her heavy duties Margaret received alarming word one day at St. Gabriel's. The army from Virginia, which had encamped at the fort built by Ingle at St. Inigoes, had grown impatient and distrustful, and was marching on St. Mary's City in a threatening mood. The informer was Edward Parker, who seemed to take a mean pleasure in giving Margaret this news, knowing she was helpless to pay the men, and feeling inwardly pleased that finally this woman who had outsmarted him years ago was now in a frightful fix.

"Unless you pay them at once," he told her, almost smiling, "they are bent on pillage and plunder."

"That's mutiny," exclaimed Margaret. "They can't do that!"

"Oh, can't they?" returned Parker scornfully. "Ah ha! They believe they have only you to deal with—a woman, and they mean business."

Margaret bit her lips, looked at Parker coldly, and said, "Is your horse tethered outside?"

"Where else, since I am here?" replied Parker in a tone of insolence.

"And here you will stay to guard all these documents and record books, keeping your nose and eyes to yourself," Margaret ordered. "I will return your horse in an hour."

Before Parker could reply, she grabbed her cloak from a peg by the door and left him to his thoughts and opinions.

She galloped down Middle Street at a furious pace seldom traveled by women on horse back, turned sharply at the Mulberry Tree onto the river road. There, a trail of dust following behind her, she met the mutineers about a mile below the Freehold.

The sight of her, alone, defenceless, unarmed, dumfounded the angry men. As one man they came to a sudden halt.

What Margaret said, what she promised, are facts history has not recorded. But the important fact, always mentioned, is that she pacified them, that they returned to their garrison

*Margaret meets the mutineers*

satisfied she would meet all their demands with justice and as quickly as might be.

Not long after this event every man was paid. Many from the Lord Baltimore's cattle or by grants of some of his land, others from Margaret's own stores of tobacco.

Leonard, as we know, had had a vote in the Assembly for himself and another as the Attorney for Lord Baltimore. Many times in the six months following his death Margaret had thought of the advantages of such a vote in the administration of the Calvert affairs, especially as she was bound to protect the interests of Leonard's heirs, William and Ann, his children and her own nephew and niece. So when the Assembly met on January 29, 1647, she appeared to ask for this "voice and vote" as executrix of Leonard's estate and as the legally appointed attorney for the Lord Baltimore.

The Assembly was horrified that a woman should make such a demand, that, for a fact, she should dare enter their meeting place. Governor Greene, shocked and dismayed, denied her petition on the spot.

But Giles was a member of the Assembly, and when he saw how matters stood he suggested that his sister should be looked upon as "his Lordship's Attorney" for recovering rights, paying debts out of the estate, and taking care of the preservation of the estate "but not further." So Governor Greene relented and decreed that "the executrix of Leonard Calvert aforesaid shall be received as his Lordship's Attorney to the intents stated by Mr. Giles Brent."

It took Margaret almost two years to settle all the matters left in her charge by Leonard's simple, five-word will. This she did to the apparent satisfaction of all in the Colony.

Then one day a ship from England brought a letter to Governor Greene from Cecilius Calvert. It was abusive, written in a furious mood, all about Margaret having dared to sell his cattle. Cecilius had not been informed of Leonard's last instructions and did not know that all this had been done to pay debts contracted for the protection of his Colony.

In turn it made the mild, ineffective Thomas Greene good and mad, too, and he immediately called the Council and read the letter to the members. Giles went straight to his sister, told her all about it, his face purple with rage and indignation. "Now," he said to Margaret, his voice very tender and loyal, "you are to drop everything, settle all your own affairs. You and I are leaving Maryland."

"You must not be hasty," Margaret told him. "No doubt there will also be a letter for me. Cecilius would not condemn me before the Governor without telling me of his action. There must be a mistake, Giles. We have been friends too long—we are doubly kin by Leonard's marriage with our sister. There will be an explanation—you wait and see."

But there was no letter for Margaret, no explanation, and definitely no mistake.

Unfortunately the Lord Baltimore's letter has been lost. Nowhere can it be found in the old records of Maryland. But the tone of it may be surmised by the reply composed by the Assembly, signed by every member, and sent to Cecilius on Saturday, April 21, 1649:

"As for Mistress Brent's undertaking and meddling with your Lordship's estates here . . . we do verily believe and in conscience report, that it was better for the Colony's safety at that time, in her hands, than in any man's else in the whole Province after your brother's death. For the soldiers would never have treated any other with that civility and respect, and though they were ready at several times to run into mutiny yet still she pacified them—till at last things were brought to that strait that she must be admitted and declared your Lordship's Attorney . . . or else all must go to ruin again. . . ."

The Assembly invited Margaret to be present when this letter to the Lord Baltimore was publicly read, approved and signed before sending. Giles and Mary went with her to St. Gabriel's and sat on either side of her during the proceedings.

When they were over many of the gentlemen of Maryland came to her individually, expressing their gratitude for all she had done for the Colony since Leonard's death. Some even went so far as to whisper to her it would have been better for Leonard to have appointed her Governor-General. Without exception everyone showed his unconcealed resentment over the injustice of the Lord Baltimore's letter.

In fact, the feeling was so bitter against Cecilius Calvert for this one piece of writing that Margaret found herself making mild excuses for him, saying he couldn't really understand the situation being so far away, and what with all his worries in disturbed England.

"But," she told everyone who came to her, "I will no longer entangle myself in Maryland, because of the Lord Baltimore's disaffection to me and the bitter invectives he has sent against me."

"Nor will I," Giles added. "My sister and I will remove to Virginia where for many years we have held tracts of land and built our separate homes against such a bitter, humiliating day as this."

"And I," Mary added quietly, "will remove myself to Kent and occupy there the manor my brother built and gave my sister who, in turn, has given it to me."

And so it was, not quite a full eleven years after they had come to St. Mary's City, that the Brents left it to its future and retired into the private life so much to their liking and preferences. And in that very year Margaret was vindicated. Cecilius Calvert, at last aware of the true conditions, sent to the Maryland Assembly the confirmation of the sale of his "neat cattle and personal estate."

Now Margaret Brent's adventures were over, and she lived for the rest of her life at Peace in Virginia.

www.ingramcontent.com/pod-product-compliance
Lightning Source LLC
LaVergne TN
LVHW021512080426
835509LV00018B/2493